248.4
Zornes 2|06

"Whether you need enc[...] to be an encourager, I e[...] encouragement by a lad[...] ...ow from personal experience to be encouragement personified."—*Jerry B. Jenkins, author of* Left Behind, Tribulation Force, Nicolae, *and a hundred other books*

"Filled with humor, hope, and encouragement, Jeanne's book brings biblical teaching on encouragement to real, everyday living. It's full of easy, practical ways to encourage folks—starting today!—*Dan Miller, polio overcomer, motivational speaker, and author of* Living, Laughing and Loving Life!

"The illustrations and examples Jeanne uses in her warm and moving book are down-to-earth, practical, and 'lived-through.' This alone makes the book one that should stir the heart of the reader to reflect on his day-to-day acting out of God's Word which adjures us to 'encourage one another.' Jeanne's book makes you think. It causes you to reflect on times when you could have helped someone and instead you passed by. I recommend this as reading for every Christian. I pray that as a result of this book, as believers express concern for each other, the world will again have to say, 'behold how they love one another.'"— *Luis Palau, evangelist and author of dozens of books including* Healthy Habits for Spiritual Growth

---

"Jeanne Zornes admits she isn't a natural-born encourager. In fact, her father nicknamed her 'Prune Juice.'" But God took her through the training of the Barnabas School and the result is this book on the art of encouragement. 'You've got a gift,' a writing teacher told her. And she does. She learned to pick daisies in a dump. And she knows how to stir a reader to long to taste the salt of another's tears, to be the touch of Jesus, to stoop to the high calling, the tender task of encouraging another human soul. Be prepared to learn how to nurture ragweeds into roses."—*Janet Chester Bly, speaker and author of dozens of books, including several series for children*

GRANT REFORMED
CHURCH LIBRARY

When I Felt like Ragweed, God Saw a ROSE

The Power of Encouragement

Jeanne Zornes

Harold Shaw Publishers
Wheaton, Illinois

Copyright © 1999 by Jeanne I. Zornes

All rights reserved. No part of this book may be reproduced or transmitted in any form or by any means, electronic or mechanical, including photocopying, recording, or any information storage and retrieval system without written permission from Harold Shaw Publishers, Box 567, Wheaton, Illinois 60189. Printed in the United States of America.

All Scripture quotations, unless otherwise indicated, are taken from the HOLY BIBLE, NEW INTERNATIONAL VERSION®. NIV®. Copyright © 1973, 1978, 1984 by International Bible Society. Used by permission of Zondervan Publishing House. All rights reserved.

The "NIV" and "New International Version" trademarks are registered in the United States Patent and Trademark Office by International Bible Society. Use of either trademark requires permission of International Bible Society.

Scripture quotations marked NASB are taken from the *New American Standard Bible,* © 1960, 1962, 1963, 1968, 1971, 1972, 1973, 1975, 1977 by The Lockman Foundation.

Scripture quotations marked KJV are taken from the King James Version of the Bible.

Cover illustration by Mary Chambers
Cover design by David LaPlaca

Library of Congress Cataloging-in-Publication Data

Zornes, Jeanne, 1947–
     [Power of encouragement]
     When I felt like ragweed, God saw a rose : the power of encouragement / Jeanne Zornes.
          p.   cm.
     Originally published: The power of encouragement. Chicago : Moody Press. © 1983.
     ISBN 0-87788-859-0 (pbk.)
     1. Encouragement.   I. Title.
BJ1475.5D63   1999
248.4—dc. 21   98-44955
                                                             CIP

03 02 01 00 99 98
10 9 8 7 6 5 4 3 2 1

*This book is for Ruth Braafladt
and Peggy Krober—
two "Barney Blooms"
in my life.*

Contents

Foreword

We all need encouragement! We all need to be given words that stimulate us to do our best for God, to fight depression, and to overcome feelings that "I can't do it!" I have been the recipient of many of those kinds of encouragement. It never ceases to amaze me how God can take someone's words and lift me into a completely different mood or way of thinking.

I remember the time I meekly confessed the frustration I was expressing toward my little daughter, and my friend acknowledged how she also became angry at her children. That gave me hope to know that I wasn't the only one. From that turning point, God began healing my anger.

I remember when my father died a neighbor brought over a meal to ease my pain. She recounted her own father's death and gave me hope to know that someday I wouldn't hurt quite as much.

I remember being discouraged about a book project I was working on. I shared my self-doubts with a writer friend. Her look of "I know exactly what you're going through" and her promise to pray for me gave me new energy to persevere.

We all know the importance of encouragement and have received its benefits. Yet at times, we feel stifled in our ability to give just the right kind of help to others. Be timid no more! The book you hold in your hands will inspire and motivate you in new ways to reach out with God's measure of courage and strength.

If you feel a lack of an ability to encourage others, Jeanne's words will give you the thrilling encouragement of "I can do this after all!" If you consider yourself a good encourager, then Jeanne's words will shower you with fresh ideas that will make you exclaim, "I never thought of doing that before." There is something for everyone in this book rich with practical ideas, warm encouragement, and uplifting honesty.

Jeanne Zornes has the wonderful ability to draw a message of useable ideas from Scripture. Though I've studied many times the passages she mentions, she gave me unique and fresh perspectives with the goal of nudging me to reach out to others through my words, writings, actions, and just listening. *When I Felt like Ragweed, God Saw a Rose* is full of clever ways to fulfill God's command to "admonish the unruly, encourage the fainthearted, help the weak, be patient with all men" (1 Thess. 5:14, NASB).

Jeanne's book will change your thinking about how important you are in the lives of others with even the most seemingly simple acts of kindness. Jeanne inspires us to bless others by speaking words, writing notes and letters, being present to listen, touching, praying, hospitality, giving, and helping. Her practical ideas, vulnerable sharing of her own life, and inspirational instruction make this book a fountain of life-giving encouragement. By the time you finish reading it, you are going to be encouraged to be an encourager.

Kathy Collard Miller, speaker and author of more than thirty-five books, including the best-selling *God's Vitamin C for the Spirit.*

Acknowledgments

A couple of blocks away from our home is an old Victorian-style home voted as having the most gorgeous yard and garden in the city. It's a flower catalog come to life. There's even a sign announcing this honor. Every day as I pass it while driving my son to high school, I admire it and dream on.

But blooms of another sort have graced my life in profusion over the last several months of this book-writing project. People have encouraged me—even as I wrote about that topic!

My thanks go first of all to my husband, Richard. As I type this, there's a rose on my desk. My husband chose his favorite—one whose creamy petals bear a blush of pink—put it in my late mother's special vase, and left it here to encourage me as I finished up the last of this book. I thank him for his patience with me as I focused on this book.

I also thank my children, Zach and Inga, who put up with Mom's telling stories on them and adjusted their homework needs for the family computer around mine.

I am grateful for those who kept asking, "When are you going to republish your first book?" and gave me courage to tackle the subject again. I'm amazed by Jan, who came into my life with a five-page letter she wrote one morning at 2:30, recounting how God had blessed her life as a "Barney." Her letter arrived just when I was about to give up on making this book a reality.

How can I thank those who prayed? Among them—Dan and Judy, Dagmar, two Karens, Marie, Georgia, Cindy, Peggy, Cheryl, Ike and Wanda, and friends from my 1997-98 Bible Study Fellowship group.

And thank you, Joan Guest, my editor at Harold Shaw Publishers, for catching the vision for this book and urging me on.

Jeanne Zornes
Psalm 71:14-15

Introduction

Bloom where you are planted.

My generation popularized that motto back in the first days of flower power, bell bottoms, and peace medallions. We believed it—that, no matter our circumstances, we could make the best of it.

Thus, when I hit the job market, I bloomed where planted. That included my summer "cub reporter" job for the daily newspaper in Tacoma, Washington. In those days, women usually hired on to write society news. I landed a slot in the Real News Room with crusty, cigar-puffing city editors as my commanders in chief.

After I'd passed the plebe tests of obituaries, tide tables, weather blurbs, and state picnic notices, they grudgingly acknowledged I was ready for a Real Story. One morning I was handed this assignment sheet: "Take a photographer to the Fox Island dump. Find out the types of good things people are throwing away. Make a good story on 'urban refusal.'"

We found the dump but few willing interviewees. Some local rats quickly slithered to obscurity. Venturing closer, I jumped at the sight of a withered green snake, which proved instead to be a deceased garden hose. Then I spotted an old rowboat, with enough leaks in its weathered hull to sink it in two minutes.

The photographer snapped a picture of me sitting in the boat (the rats refused to pose), and we were off. I turned in a humorous story, which hit page A-9 with photo, was picked up by a national magazine, and earned me—for the rest of the summer—the dubious title of "Garbage Editor."

It's not always easy to pick daisies in a dump. In both school and work worlds, I encountered withered people who spread discontent and disharmony. But God had a different training program for me. He replanted me in other environments, pruned me through difficult times, watered me with his Word, and poured the light of his love into my life. Then God assigned me to share what I'd learned. A master's thesis on communicating encouragement became a real book, *The Power of Encouragement*. First published in 1981, it sold for a decade, an unusual thing for a first book from an unknown writer. It had to be the Lord's doing . . . and his sovereign desire to get this message out.

When the book went out of print, people continued to write me for copies. I was down to the last twenty when the Lord planted a new seed in my heart: to plow the old encouragement garden and replant. The result is this revised book, encouraging people again to become encouragers.

If you read the first, I think you'll enjoy reading this one. Fifteen more years of living and watching encouragement happen are sprinkled through its pages. If you never read the first, I'm so glad you have this one in your hands. My prayer is that God will encourage you to bloom where he has planted you.

1

Barney Blooms

The Traits of the Encourager

It was a dark and stormy night in the City of Roses as some shadowy figures crept to predetermined office doors.

And you thought this was a nonfiction book!

Ah, but the mystery people were "The Barnabas Committee." Their few weeks' clandestine work changed at least one life forever. Mine!

But this story really began more than a dozen years earlier as I grew up in the Generation of the Discontented. My college peers marked the sixties with Vietnam protests, racial unrest, student rights, and the explosion of drug problems. I didn't pull a cause off those shelves, but I had a hard time finding my niche. After working for a newspaper and then as a writer with Wycliffe Bible Translators, I made a radical turn in my life. Pulling together my life savings, I enrolled in a one-year intensive Bible course in Portland, Oregon. I thought studying the Bible all day would be the next best thing to heaven!

Whoever said, "Into each life a little rain must fall" surely hadn't lived in Portland, "City of Roses." Its first autumn drizzles coincided with a flood of college homework. Plus, after living alone for several years, "home" became the bottom bunk in a college apartment shared with three other women. I signed up for voice lessons and came down with big-time strep throat. My trusty old car turned into an expensive hypochondriac with carburetor and battery problems. My already-tight finances got tighter than a shrunk girdle.

Problems loomed 150 miles away at home, too. Dad's company forced him into an early retirement with reduced pension. Mom, with her bad bones, fell down the stairs and broke her ankle. Then her cancer, once beaten with a mastectomy, returned to her liver.

Back on campus, I felt like a pile of wilted ragweed. I also noticed gloom clutching other students and staff. It seemed that Bible school was a favorite target of the Author of Discouragement. I'd read C. S. Lewis's *The Screwtape Letters,* in which a devil advises a junior tempter named Wormwood. I imagined him dancing down our sidewalks and commending Wormwood, "Well done, thou bad and faithful tempter. You're splendidly distracting these Bible school humans from the purposes of our Enemy."

But God is bigger than any gloomy problem. He began to show me that one chilly morning as I dragged into a first-period class in the Gospels. Our professor, fresh out of seminary and working on his doctorate, had struggled to keep ahead of multiple class preparations. Many nights, as I walked home from the library, I'd see his office light on and his head bent over his desk. We'd noticed his lectures weren't polished, but hey—we were all still learning.

That morning, he began class by asking for our understanding and forgiveness for his inadequate preparations over the past few weeks. He requested prayers for his overwhelming work load. Then, hands shaking, he put on his glasses and started the lecture.

The class was stunned by his courage to admit a need. I wanted to do something positive, but what?

Encouragement 101

My response was "The Barnabas Committee," named for the New Testament's "Son of Encouragement." A handful of students agreed to join me in praying for and encouraging this professor and other faculty and staff. We didn't want to embarrass people nor come across as the Brownie Point Bunch. So we decided to stay anonymous.

We communicated our concern and love through little typed notes of encouragement, sometimes in silly rhyme, that were signed simply "The Barnabas Committee." Often we attached gifts such as candy bars, apples, or animal crackers. We sent these encouragement parcels through the campus mail or sneaked around campus at night to leave them by office doors. We had no idea what prolific blooms we had planted in the "glooms." Many sent the committee little thank-you notes. This frustrated the campus mail clerk, who didn't know which campus postal box belonged to the "committee"! She turned them over to the school bulletin lady, who sandwiched them between announcements for classroom changes and soccer practice times.

Our "anonymous" ministry now had an air of mystery. Who, students started wondering, was "The Barnabas Committee"? Especially when whatever they were doing inspired such poetic gems as this, responding to a May basket of suckers left for the weekly faculty meeting:

> Each one of us, dear Barnabas,
> Finds our vest buttons hopping,
> Not only for the pride of you,
> But calories—lollipopping.
> Our "pulchritude," our "attitude,"
> Our "fortitude," our tickers,
> Were touched, enhanced and blessed
> By your bag full of lickers.
> —The Faculty

We started noticing others pick up the message: *"Encourage one another."* People started telling and showing others they cared. It seemed to us that the campus mood turned back to positive. Most amazing was this: as we focused on encouraging others, we were encouraged ourselves. Our problems didn't go away, but we quit focusing on them and instead looked to God's goodness and promises.

Graduation brought an end to The Barnabas Committee. At commencement, as I walked across the stage in front of faculty, I stifled the urge to wink at all those who'd been the target of my "encourager" misdeeds!

Encouragement 102

Little did I know how God had greater plans for the originator of The Barnabas Committee. On a June morning a year later, I got a phone call at work. "Come quickly," my dad pleaded. "Your mother may not last the night." I knew, outside of a miracle, I'd someday get that call. But this was Mom. I wanted her to live to see me marry, cuddle my babies, and be my best friend. Not die.

Somehow, on that chilly, rainy, dreary day I found the strength to drive three hours to the hospital where she lay unconscious. Together as a family we held her hands and heard Dad read Psalm 116 to her.

> I love the Lord, because he hath heard my voice
>> and my supplications.
> Because he hath inclined his ear unto me,
>> therefore will I call upon him as long as I live.

A nurse came, dabbed her lips with moisture, injected more painkiller, squeezed our shoulders, spoke softly and compassionately, and left to give us privacy in our wait.

> Precious in the sight of the Lord
>> is the death of his saints. (Ps. 116:1-2, 15, KJV)

My mother died early the next morning. I hurt for her suffering. I hurt for my dad's loss. And I hurt. I'd planned to start graduate work in Illinois at the end of the summer.

But seeing my dad's devastation broke my heart. I wondered if I should abandon those plans and live with him that first tough year. But close friends and the family urged me to go ahead with my plans. Others would be there for my father.

So, late in August, I packed my typewriter and clothes into the car. Dad's good-bye hug was heavy and sorrowful. As I headed east, I could hardly see through the tears to drive.

The demands of graduate school made Bible school seem like sandbox play. I struggled to keep up as I also worked through my grief. I wrote my dad at least a postcard once or twice a week. I called a few times, but he choked up and couldn't talk. I didn't know how else to encourage him.

Then came a second phone call, the second week of my second quarter in school. Dad was dead of a heart attack. And my life would never be the same.

Dad had wanted me to settle his affairs, something he confirmed when he put my name on his checking account and showed me his will and other papers. Still single at thirty-one, I was more mobile and "available" than my married sister, who had two small children, owned a business, and lived on the other side of the state.

Dropping out of school, I moved home from Illinois and began sorting through my parents' belongings, holding garage sales, painting the house, cleaning up the yard, and slogging through the paperwork of probate. I just wanted to finish what I had to do and get on with life. With each yard sale, my parents' home was less "home." Although I'd spent half my childhood within its walls, I'd lived the previous decade in six other cities. Here I had no close friends and no church home.

It was the toughest year of my life. For the previous four years, I had the spiritual support of godly people through my mission service, Bible college, and work for a Christian publisher. Now I was alone, aware that people who didn't share my faith were watching how I coped with grief and discouragement. I wanted to do it right. As the months dragged on, however, the burden grew oppressive. Sometimes I wondered if I'd ever find a way out of my circumstances. I doubted my self-worth and questioned my purpose in life. My sister's family and work gave her many good reasons to live. But I was so low that sometimes I found myself asking, What about me? Am I really needed? I wasn't a quitter, and that kept me plodding through the clean-out and probate process. As I look back, I know people stepped in to encourage me. But my needs were so deep I saw little beyond my present difficulties.

Back to the Basics

My old bedroom became my oasis from the clutter of clean-out and the house's haunting memories. I sat on my bed, reading the Bible with more earnestness than ever before as I sought comfort. That first winter, as I retraced my way from Genesis to Revelation, I repeatedly marked verses as God seemed to say, "Here, this is encouragement." I'd once pigeonholed "encouragement" as just a "spiritual gift" listed in Romans 12:8. Now I saw threads of caring running liberally throughout all the fabric of Scripture.

I realized that encouragement involved many "gifts" or special, Spirit-endowed abilities. It could be communicated in a multitude of ways. Above all, it required a living, growing faith within a living, growing Body—the church. I was reminded of the statement by martyred German pastor Dietrich Bonhoeffer: "Do we really think there is a single person in this world who does not need either encouragement or admonition? Why, then, has God bestowed Christian brotherhood on us?"[1]

Pure and simple, God created us to need him and each other. We need to encourage one another because our sin-tainted world delights in discouragement. Negative people can pollute our outlook; negative circumstances, our hope.

The real battlefield of life's tough times is spiritual. We need each other to keep our faith and hope strong. Hebrews 3:13 says just that: "But encourage one another daily, as long as it is called Today, so that none of you may be hardened by sin's deceitfulness."

Reading again in Acts, I realized the namesake for my Bible school "encourager committee" had a more profound message than I'd earlier seen. As I pieced together his biography, I found six traits that fit into the acronym FRIEND. He was

- free in Christ
- responsive
- iron hearted
- encouraging
- nurturing
- deferential

Free in Christ

Barnabas was the sunflower of the New Testament—strong, tall, and cheerful. Named Joseph when born on the island of Cyprus, he traced his ancestry to the Levites, the tribe of priests God appointed to take care of Israel's worship system. When he came to Jerusalem and connected with the followers of Jesus, he got a nickname, Barnabas, meaning "son of encouragement" or "son of consolation." His new "tag" probably honored him as a man whose secure walk with Christ enabled him to make and keep friends. He lived out John 8:36: "So if the Son sets you free, you will be free indeed." Possibly he had a positive, outgoing personality. When I was a little girl, my dad nicknamed me "Prune Juice," probably for a sour streak to my personality. I surely didn't appreciate it! But as I look back, I realize my parents were just trying to remind me that negative people didn't make very good friends. Imagine your friends calling you "Encourager." If that doesn't make you want to go out and paint the world bright colors, nothing will!

I often wonder if Barnabas was a big happy guy with a healthy "holy hug." Scripture hints at him being large and loud. When he and Paul went to Lystra on the first missionary journey (Acts 14), the local people mistook them for gods. They hailed articulate Paul as Hermes, a god who conveyed messages for other gods. They decided Barnabas was thunder-throated Zeus, their most prominent deity. But Barnabas didn't go along with the presumption. He considered himself just an ordinary guy serving an extraordinary God and expressed his faith with energy and joy.

We follow Barnabas's example when we celebrate life. Because people are important to us in Christ, we're there for them at life's change points. We weep with those who weep and especially laugh with those who laugh. I think of Peggy, who had a knack for showing love through the outrageous. When I faced a not-too-welcome midlife birthday, Peggy kidnapped me and took me to our town's Riverfront Park. She plopped a cone-shaped party hat on me, spread out a tablecloth with nice china, and proceeded to serve baked eggs and fruit for a birthday breakfast. Before that first forkful, she prayed for me. Did our little party ever entertain the joggers passing by that July morning! As we laughed, I realized here was somebody who'd never call me "Prune Juice"! She was my "Barnabas Buddy."

Responsive

Say "true blue" and I think first of a hydrangea bush that bloomed right outside my childhood bedroom window. The years it was given the proper fertilizer it exploded with clusters of those blue pompon flowers. Years later, when I had an economy wedding with flowers from a friend's garden, I had blue hydrangea tied together for my bridal bouquet. To me, the color denoted the loyalty I'd need to cultivate in marriage with listening ears and a sensitive heart. Yet I'm the first to admit I haven't arrived in that department. My family claims I have tunnel hearing: what they say goes right in one ear and out the other. Uh-huh. Sure. Well, I'm working on it. But I get so preoccupied that I often fail to give the other person my total, caring attention.

Not Barnabas. He modeled how to respond as a true-blue listener. One day he encountered a religious outcast named Saul. Nobody trusted him. A short time before, he'd been terrorizing Christians. Now he was back in town telling people he was a Christian. The apostles were skeptical. Given Saul's track record, he could be spying or setting traps. But Barnabas sat down and really listened to the guy. Then he took Saul back to the apostles and retold his testimony (Acts 9:27). This time the church leaders were more accepting and took Saul in.

A few years later, Barnabas and Saul (renamed Paul) were a famous missionary team. They were getting ready for their second major missionary journey when Barnabas asked to take his cousin John Mark along. He saw in the young man an uncut gem, perhaps another Paul. But Paul refused. John Mark had deserted them earlier, and Paul didn't want to go through that again.

Neither would yield, and they split. Paul left with Silas. Barnabas stuck with John Mark, forfeiting a possibly famous role in shaping the New Testament church. But his decision to encourage John Mark bore fruit. From that young man came the Gospel of Mark. Just before dying, the great apostle admitted that Mark had been useful in ministry (2 Tim. 4:11)—all because Barnabas listened and got involved.

James 1:19 says we should be quick to listen and slow to speak. That's why God created us with two ears and only one mouth! The person who has learned the art of listening is the one who is willing to take time with those for whom others don't have patience.

Iron Hearted
The pansies by my driveway are my "Comeback Kids." Every winter they suffocate under the pile of snow shoveled

off the driveway. Every spring I think I've lost them. But as days get warmer, they come alive and spread with ever greater showiness. Their endurance reminds me of a marathon our valley sponsors every year called "Ridge to River." Most people team up for the race's skiing, running, biking, and kayaking. A few, called Iron Men, ripple their muscles and go it alone. By the time they cross the finish line, the rest of us are reminded to pay a little more attention to our own physical fitness!

Proverbs 27:17 says, "As iron sharpens iron, so one man sharpens another." An encourager is an iron man, challenging us to become more, better, and deeper. That's what Barnabas did for Saul. Saul was making so many enemies that he literally became a basket case, lowered over the wall of Damascus to escape would-be murderers. Saul returned to his hometown, Tarsus, and dropped out of the headlines. But Barnabas never forgot him. A few years later, Acts 11:25 reveals, Barnabas made a special side trip to Tarsus to find Saul, then took him back to Antioch, where he trained Saul for ministry. One iron man putting another would-be iron man through the disciplines.

Barnabas also encouraged and inspired large groups of people. When the Jerusalem church sent him to Antioch to check out rumors that Gentiles had become Christians, "he was glad and encouraged them all to remain true to the Lord with all their hearts" (Acts 11:23). Later, teamed with Saul-renamed-Paul, and preaching in churches they had started in Asia Minor, Barnabas's ministry involved "strengthening the disciples and encouraging them to remain true to the faith" (Acts 14:22).

How can we be iron people? By encouraging others to become "comeback kids" and to never give up growing. Some "iron women" pushed me beyond novice homemaking by teaching me to sew T-shirts, can peaches, and organize files. Simple stuff—but mastering those skills gave me courage to try more difficult life skills. Others encouraged me intellectually, recommending good books and sharing articles of mutual interest. Still others challenged me spiritually. I remember Gary, whose standard greeting was "How are you doing spiritually?" He meant it, and we recalled his concern when tall, athletic Gary, barely forty, one Easter morning dropped dead of a congenital heart problem.

Encouraging

A generous friend gave us a start of one of nature's most generous bulb flowers, the grape hyacinth. With generous spontaneity (are you getting the "generous" message?), those purple-beaded stalks pop out alongside nearly every flower in my beds. With similar diligence, Barnabas was a "come-along-sider." Like a tugboat aiding a ship to dock, he simply "drew alongside" dozens, perhaps hundreds, for the Lord. That is the literal idea of the Greek word *paraklesis,* which means "encouragement." The same root word is used in John 15 to describe the Holy Spirit as the Comforter.

I experienced "coming alongside" one morning at graduate school while studying in my second-floor apartment. Looking down, I noticed another student struggling with a heavy suitcase, fat pillow, bulging book bag, and purse. I presumed she was trying to get to the train depot, a few blocks away. I looked at my clock and realized the train was due in ten minutes. She'd never make it alone. I couldn't keep studying. I grabbed my keys, ran out the door, and caught up with her.

"Headed to the train?" I asked, taking the pillow and book bag. We ran together the remaining blocks and arrived just as the train whistled up. As I jogged home I found I had renewed energy to study—and not just from the run. God had encouraged me as I obeyed his command to encourage someone else.

Barnabas fulfilled a similar role in approaching and helping people in need. His first recorded act in Scripture was selling a tract of land and donating the amount for distribution among needy believers (Acts 4:37). It's possible that land was his insurance policy against lean times. But Barnabas had a giving heart and was trusting God for anything he might need in the future.

It's humbling to be around giving people. I know, from the years people sent money for my missionary support and later to help me through Bible college and graduate school. I'm not the only one who's been blessed that way. Moreover, giving isn't limited to money. We encourage when we share sacrificially of anything we could claim as our own. God may ask us to share the food in our cupboards, the gas in our cars, the extra bed (or even our own), or the time we want to keep all to ourselves.

Nurturing

My husband's late uncle loved to grow begonias, a fussy, shade-loving flower with velvety petals in neon colors. These flowers took a tremendous amount of nurturing. Barnabas, too, was a nurturer. Acts 11:24 simply but profoundly calls Barnabas "a good man, full of the Holy Spirit and faith." Because he was secure in his relationship with Christ, he could reach out to cheer and encourage those still stumbling spiritually.

You don't teach somebody to swim if you can't swim yourself. You don't encourage and build up new Christians if you don't know the Lord in a personal, vital way. You must be in God's Word regularly, applying it to your own life, in order to nurture others. You must be quiet enough in your own spirit to hear the direction of the Lord.

The year after Bible college I met Meg, a self-admitted hippie with a wobbly new faith. The churches nearby were too "straight" for her. She agreed to do a Bible study with me and another girl but only came twice. She claimed her brain was too messed up from drugs to concentrate on the Bible. Yet I knew she'd soon stumble in her faith walk without God's Word.

"Meg," I said, "I don't expect you to understand everything you're reading. But let God's Word flow through you, like water running through a sieve. It will help clean out all the ugly stuff that's been there all these years."

At first I doubted she'd take my advice. We moved away and lost touch for a while. Then I learned that Meg was a missionary candidate. Others had moved into her life and nurtured her to a steady walk with Christ and a commitment to God's Word.

Deferential

I welcome my spring show of crocuses, daffodils, and tulips. But when their season is past, their leaves wither as they "defer" to other plantings for the summer. A person who defers to another submits or yields to that person. He or she has a servant's heart. That was the greatest characteristic of Barnabas. He expected no glory for his efforts.

We see that in his relationship with Paul. As they teamed up for evangelistic work, Paul started to outshine his mentor. We pick that up from the order in which he and Paul (called Saul until Acts 13:9) are named in accounts of their mission work. In Acts 11:30, "Barnabas and Saul" were assigned to deliver a famine relief offering. In Acts 12:25, "Barnabas and Saul" returned from that task. In Acts 13:1-2, Barnabas headed the list of potential missionary appointees, with Saul coming last. It is the same order when they went to Paphos and met the proconsul (Acts 13:7).

But that first missionary trip marked a change. After their work in Cyprus they sailed across the Mediterranean and started through Asia Minor. At Pisidian Antioch, Paul preached a sermon that rocked the city. Note Acts 13:42, NASB: "And as Paul and Barnabas were going out, the people kept begging that these things might be spoken to them the next Sabbath." No longer was it "Barnabas and Saul." Paul took leadership and prominence. Throughout the rest of Acts, with only one exception (Acts 14:14), Paul was the number one man. Barnabas didn't demand equal billing as God blessed Paul's ministry. He quietly stepped aside to let God work.

Deference requires humility, a willingness to be put aside if that's God's best plan. F. B. Meyer, a famous London preacher, learned that as he aged and somebody named G. Campbell Morgan became a frequent pulpit guest. Meyer had always drawn the crowds when he came to America to preach. But now people wanted to hear Morgan. Instead of resenting the change, he went to prayer. Later he was seen going about town saying, "Have you heard G. Campbell Morgan? God gifted him." Not surprisingly, Meyer once remarked that if he had his life to live over, he'd spend more time in the ministry of encouragement.

That's what God is calling each of us to do. He wants us there as cheerleaders, willing to put another's needs and success ahead of our own. When we can do that, then we can humbly and nobly carry the designation "Sons and Daughters of Encouragement."

I now live 250 miles northeast of the City of Roses. But I have my own roses alongside our driveway. All winter, they're dead and ugly. In April, they're pruned so cruelly that they look like a jungle booby trap. Then my husband pours on foul-smelling concoctions. In early spring, there's nothing "rosy" about them. But by June, when the first buds burst off healthy stems, the season of glory begins.

Those roses symbolize the ministry of encouragement. We'll inevitably have ugly times in our lives. We'll be downcast, thinking ourselves incapable of anything worthy or beautiful. But Hebrews 10:24-25 points us to this hope: "Let us consider how we may spur one another on toward love and good deeds. Let us not give up meeting together, as some are in the habit of doing, but let us encourage one another—and all the more as you see the Day approaching." God prunes us toward "love and good deeds" through life's hardships. He provides his Word to be water, and nurturing, affirming people to be fertilizer. He floods us with his Son's light as we anticipate the Event of the Ages—the encouraging knowledge that Jesus is coming again.

Until then, we're to be at work spurring one another to love and good deeds. That's encouragement. In the rest of this book, you'll discover eight ways to become a "Barney Bloom": speaking, writing, presence, touch, prayer, hospitality, giving, and helping. Bring on the rain and get ready for the flowers!

Groomed to Bloom

1. Look back through the FRIEND traits of Barnabas. How are you doing in each?
   F (Free in Christ): Are you friendly and fun?
   R (Responsive): Do you talk less and listen more?
   I (Iron-hearted): Do you help people better themselves?
   E (Encouraging): Do you regularly come alongside people in need?
   N (Nurturing): Are you growing spiritually?
   D (Deferential): Do you cheer others to success?
2. Proverbs 17:17 says, "A friend loves at all times." When might it be hard to love?
3. Skim Hebrews 11, the "Roll Call of Faith" chapter. What rewards in this life did these people receive for their ministries?
4. Someone once said, "Giving is its own reward." How would that apply to the ministry of encouragement?
5. An effective ministry of encouragement has God's Word as its heart. Each chapter of this study will suggest a verse to put in your heart through memorization. This one will remind you to bloom where you are planted:

   "I consider everything a loss compared to the surpassing greatness of knowing Christ Jesus my Lord" (Phil. 3:8).

2
The Bent Bloom Cure

The Encouragement of Spoken Words

Next time you want to know the truth, the real truth, and nothing but the truth about plants, visit a school science fair. All the world's future Gregor Mendels and Luther Burbanks will regale you with stories of bean plants that grew and ones that didn't . . . and why. Some day, one young scientist will solve the mystery of the ages: the connection between plant growth and music. We've already learned that cows are more contented with Bach than rock. But the jury is still out on the musical tastes of beans.

At least that's what I concluded as I wandered the aisles of the Foothills Middle School science fair. A dutiful mother, I first visited my son's study of aerodynamics, including a wind tunnel outfitted with his portable bedroom fan. I poured on the praise, leaving his ego in a high flight pattern. Then it was on to the botany exhibits, where I spotted the perennial adolescent science project: "Plant A was exposed to classical music. Plant B was exposed to country western music. Plant C was exposed to hard rock music. All plants received equal amounts of sun and water. My results are inconclusive."

Those bent and droopy experimental plants reminded me of a slightly wacky friend who claimed speaking kindly to her plants helped them grow better. I'll confess I spoke harshly to one of the house plants that I inherited when I married. Ceiling-high "Phil," the philodendron, had the plant version of inner ear dysfunction and would fall over quite loudly in the middle of the night. Phil never did look perky and even less so when we pawned it off on an unsuspecting friend.

I'm not sure if we'll ever answer the relationship between plants and the quality of sound waves reaching them, be they music or words. But I do know how the human variety of young shoots and mature trees that inhabit our home unbend and bloom to harmonious sounds—the ones known as verbal encouragement. Even Mark Twain once remarked that he could live three weeks on a compliment!

People who reach out with words of encouragement are like fertilizer and sunshine to struggling plants. They fulfill the principle of Proverbs 16:24: "Pleasant words are a honeycomb, sweet to the soul and healing to the bones." Yet words can also be destructive: "Death and life are in the power of the tongue" (Prov. 18:21, NASB). We're often like the cowboy who rode up to two grazing buffalo. "You are the ugliest animals I've ever seen!" he shouted. "Your fur is matted, you have big humps on your backs, and just look at how you drool!" As the cowboy kicked his horse and galloped off, one buffalo turned to the other and said, "I think I just heard a discouraging word." He could at least have told those old buffalo that their hides made great sleigh robes.

"Out of the same mouth," says James 3:10, "come praise and cursing." We make the choice. People all around us need the lift of verbal encouragement. We're God's messengers for the hope expressed in Psalm 40:1-3:

> I waited patiently for the LORD; he turned to me and heard my cry.
> He lifted me out of the slimy pit, out of the mud and mire;
> he set my feet on a rock and gave me a firm place to stand.

He put a new song in my mouth, a hymn of praise to our God.

This passage reminds us that verbal encouragers

- reach out to people,
- lift people up, and
- anchor people spiritually.

Reacher-Outers

Psalm 40:1 reminds me of the account in the book of Jeremiah of one of the last wicked kings of Judah throwing the prophet Jeremiah in a muddy cistern. Jeremiah 38:6 says, "Jeremiah sank down into the mud." That's an understatement! Jeremiah would have either starved or suffocated in that fetid pit.

But he had a "reacher-outer," a compassionate palace official named Ebed-Melech. This man risked the king's temper by suggesting Jeremiah's punishment was cruel and unfair. I can imagine Jeremiah's amazement after possibly days in that stinky, foul mess when this official hollered down, "We're going to pull you out."

Reacher-outers take risks to address a negative situation. Often, we think of kind words we could say to someone, but we let the opportunity pass by. We shouldn't. We might be just the person God needs to minister to the other person.

I remember one frigid night in Chicago, where I lived before I married. I'd put on long underwear, settled into a rocker, and wrapped a thick afghan around me as the wind outside whipped the snow to a chill factor of forty-five degrees below zero. There was an icy spot in my heart, too, from an unkind remark somebody made that day. Then my phone rang. Reluctantly, I unwrapped myself. Most likely it was another wrong number for the popular coed at the nearby college whose number got mixed up with mine.

"Keeping warm?" my caller asked. Quickly I recognized

a voice from twenty-four hundred miles away. My former neighbor in Washington state, hearing a report on Chicago's cold, had called just to see how I was doing. An old Japanese proverb says, "One kind word can warm three winter months." Believe me, her call cheered, encouraged, and warmed me up.

That same neighbor boosted me as I cleaned out my parents' home after their deaths. She always had a compliment when she called or stopped by. "You've really arranged this garage sale nicely," she'd say. Or, "The yard is looking so sharp." "I can't believe how fast you painted that room." "You're really conscientious with that probate work." I needed to hear those comments, for they reminded me I was valuable to God and had purpose beyond the tasks of death.

People all around us need an encouraging word. As a college student, Pat was discouraged over his studies and finances. One day, leaving a history lecture, he was stopped by a Christian professor. "I've been watching you, and you look really down," the professor said. "I'm wondering what's the matter. Don't forget, you're not here by accident. God led you here, and he will see you through." Years later, Pat practiced similar sensitivity as a chaplain holding services for a professional baseball team. Noticing a player seemed especially down, he chatted with the man and mentioned his daughter-in-law was a long-time fan.

"You don't know what that means," the surprised player said. "Just this morning I decided to quit." Pat praised the player's ability, encouraged him to stay in pro ball, and promised to pray for him. The next week, the player wrote that he was encouraged to stay on the team.

Encouragement can lighten the load at the work place. Executives especially need to take the lead in affirming employees. A secretary typed her way through dictation a boss mailed in from a business trip. At the end she heard, "Thanks very much for doing these letters, Mary. I don't know how I'd get along without you, even though I don't say it very often." The secretary remarked: "I've been typing faster for three weeks, on the strength of that word of praise!"[1]

Employees in service industries also need a good word. They usually get only negative feedback and will long remember a positive remark. It's also a great way to show Christ's love to nonbelievers as well as encourage those who share the faith. When my very full grocery cart includes lots of processing challenges, like double coupons, I hand over my payment with a smile and sincere compliment for the checker's super job. Because my checks have Bible verses printed on them, I dare not do otherwise! When we had new carpet put in our home, we commended the excellent carpet layer before he left. Then my husband called the carpet store manager and said, "Thanks for sending your best man out to our home. He did a wonderful job." One Christian college coach remembers how a student practiced affirmation at meal stops on game trips. The student never left without asking to see the manager—to thank him, the cook, and the waitress for service rendered to a roomful of hungry young men.

Lifter-Uppers

Back to Jeremiah. The cistern's mud was slowly swallowing him alive. Ebed-Melech threw down rags and old clothes to pad Jeremiah's arm pits from the rope. Then thirty men pulled hard to extract him from the jaws of the earth. Ouch!

Sometimes, when God asks us to be verbal "lifter-uppers," we have to pull hard. People may be so down on themselves that they can't believe there's hope ahead. They may be so entrenched in personal sorrow that they feel stuck forever. Yet God calls us to throw down the ropes, then dig in our feet to pull them out and lift them up.

We especially need to practice this type of affirmation in our homes. Our parents, mates, and children will bloom a lot brighter when they hear they're important and cherished. Children seem to particularly respond to verbal affirmation—maybe because they hear "no" too often.

"In many little ways," writes Dorothy Briggs in *Your Child's Self-Esteem,* "we forget to focus on the unique gifts of each child. We focus on what he doesn't have. When we habitually attend to what's missing, cherishing gets lost. If your child lacks faith in himself or herself, search to find what he or she can do. Give plenty of recognition for those things and refuse to focus on what he or she cannot do. A child's sense of success—victory—is the key to self-confidence. It feeds the child's conviction that he or she has something to offer, which spurs the child on to new efforts."[2] Years ago, when my nephew David was five years old, I visited at Christmas and watched him create a special gift for his father. He glued four rocks on a plank from the firewood pile, then drew faces on the rocks to represent his family. It was a major effort for a little guy who lived in the shadow of a do-all older sister. On Christmas Day, his gift was greeted with lots of positive remarks and hugs. As guests came through for the holidays, his mother made sure they saw David's project. "And he did it all by himself," she boasted loudly so he could overhear.

I remembered that incident when I became a mother and realized my children's creative efforts were part of their self-esteem. That's why I sat down and let my son, Zach, explain every detail of his latest model-building project, saying "Wow! Great job!" several different ways. And when my daughter, Inga, showed me progress on her latest hemp-and-bead necklace, I told her what a wonderfully clever child she was. Homework time can also become encouragement time: "That story is so creative! How did you think of such wonderful figures of speech?" "Your deductive skills are top-notch. I wouldn't have known how to solve that algebra problem."

One of my former pastors said his family sometimes used dinner times to single out one member for special affirmation. "All of us have to tell at least one good thing we like about that person," he said. "An hour before dinner the kids may have been fighting with each other. But when dinner comes they know they'll have to say something positive. They'll have to admit, 'He's neat' or 'She's kind.'" He and his wife also affirmed displays of positive character, especially in their relationships with others. "I saw what you did for your sister, and I appreciated that," he might say to a child. "It really showed character."

And don't forget your mate. Love thrives on positive words. Try the verbal bouquets that start out, "I love how you . . ." or "It means so much to me that you . . ." We get in ruts of just living with one another, failing to verbalize why someone we love is special. I learn from my husband in those areas. I'm not exactly Julia Child in the kitchen, but when he savors a dinner and says, "You got that salmon just right," I don't mind washing dishes afterwards for half an hour. Or when I've put six piles of laundry back on beds and in closets and drawers, the weariness of housework fades when I hear, "I really appreciate how you don't let the dirty clothes pile up." Similarly, my kids need to hear (within their dad's earshot): "Your dad works so hard to support our family."

Encouragement can keep a person from quitting. I play a halfway decent violin, thanks to a lifter-upper strings teacher in public school. When I started violin in seventh grade, most of my friends had already been playing for three years. As a beginner, I was buried in the balcony of the second violin section. Although I knew how to read music from piano lessons, my fingers felt like thumbs and my bow duplicated the screech of a braking locomotive. As I tearfully practiced at home, our family's two Siamese cats roamed the house yowling their protest. (I suspect my playing sounded like a cat in heat!) One day, when my string teacher took me aside to check my progress, my frustration exploded in tears. He looked at me kindly and said, "I know you want to play well, and I want you to know you're doing just great. You've really improved fast. Just keep in there. I'm proud of you." That affirmation kept me hoping and practicing. Five years later I sat as concertmistress of the high school orchestra.

There's more evidence of this in a story Franklin Graham, oldest son of Billy Graham, tells in his autobiography. Evangelist John Wesley White came into Franklin's life as a friend and adviser at a time when Franklin was heading up Samaritan's Purse, a Christian relief group. Franklin had long fought being pushed into a certain mold as the oldest son of the famous evangelist. But John finally convinced Franklin to share speaking at some crusades. "More than anything else," Franklin wrote, "John was an encourager. Every time I stood up to preach, during my message he would say out loud, 'Good point, Franklin,' or 'That's good.' Some people might think that would be distracting, but it was a comfort knowing I had a friend like that with me."[3]

Sometimes I solve the awkwardness of verbal encouragement by prefacing my remark with one of these phrases: "I really appreciate how you . . . ," "It means so much to me that you . . . ," or "I like the way that you . . ." One time I told a nurse, "I've always appreciated the way nurses help ease both physical and emotional pain." That prompted her to recall an incident that left her feeling positive about herself. I told another woman, "I could use some hints from an experienced mother like you in helping my children keep their rooms clean." After nearly fainting over the adjective *experienced,* she shared even more ideas that confirmed her reputation as a homemaker.

Other times it helps to precede a remark with, "Can I be serious and tell you something about you?" Or, "At the risk of embarrassing you, I'd like to tell you something very special." One day I told a pastor, "You may think this sounds strange, but I just want to thank you for the way you sometimes preach through tears. It shows me you're a man who really cares." I think I saw him bloom a little brighter.

Sometimes we're called to praise a situation that hasn't quite "arrived." Several years ago I picked up a sheet called "100 Ways for 4-H Judges to Say 'Very Good.'" I wish I could paste it on my forehead for constant referral! Among the suggestions:

> "You're on the right track now."
> "Good for you!"
> "Nothing can stop you now!"
> "That's the best ever."
> "That's better than ever."
> "Couldn't have done better myself."
> "Now that's what I call a fine job!"
> "I like that."
> "It's a pleasure to teach when you work like that."
> "You've got your brain in gear today."

Spiritual Anchors

When Jeremiah crawled out of that slimy cistern, I imagine him straightening his back, then stomping his muddy feet around the wonderfully solid ground of the guards' court-yard. Similarly, verbal affirmation not only reaches down and lifts up people but sends them off with firm footsteps.

Not all encouragement is what people regard as positive strokes. The Greek word for encouragement, *paraklesis*, means both "comfort" and "exhortation." We comfort when we cover negatives with grace. We exhort when we help a person turn existing or potential negatives into positives. It's a delicate balance, for not everyone appreciates being told he or she is headed in the wrong direction. Yet Proverbs 17:10 reminds us of the potential of verbal re-alignment: "A rebuke impresses a man of discernment more than a hundred lashes a fool." That rebuke must be tempered with love. Paul told Timothy to "correct, rebuke and encourage—with great patience and careful instruction" (2 Tim. 4:2). Only love can prevent exhortation from becoming a negative criticism that wounds without healing.

"The spirit of a Christless society is to gossip, ridicule, focus on mistakes, and emphasize weaknesses of leaders," John Alexander wrote in *Practical Criticism*. "Our nation is riddled with critics who can point out what's wrong with nary a word of how to make it better. Rare indeed is the individual who can temper the indictment with a commensurate dose of viable options."[4] It's far better to partner criticism with remedial suggestions. Our natural tendency is just to tell people what they should stop doing and start doing. But the encourager goes one step further, telling them what they should continue doing and better ways of doing that.

The apostle Paul did a lot of the same as he exhorted believers in the early church. His letters repeatedly started with praise for their walk of faith. He urged them to "live a life worthy of the calling you have received" (Eph. 4:1). But he also exhorted them to turn away from choices that didn't honor God. He "edited" the Corinthians, for example, regarding worldliness, immorality, and infighting, then gave them a new goal: "Our prayer is for your perfection" (2 Cor. 13:9). We participate in that spirit of encouragement when we prayerfully guide people to God's call on their lives.

Nearly a year after my father's death, I sat across from the lawyer who'd guided me through every last document for probate. The work was done—except for selling the house in a depressed housing market. We didn't want to turn the clean, buyer-ready house into a rental or leave it sitting empty. Though I wanted to get on with my life and finish graduate studies, I felt I had no alternatives but to stay and wait. As we closed the files, this Christian lawyer, old enough to be my father, switched hats to encourager and said, "I think you should go back to school. Let God take care of these details." His statement of faith in me and in God's provision proved right. Two weeks later I was back at school. A spot opened for me in housing within three days, when a sick student dropped out. The house didn't sell until I'd finished my graduate work. But it was never vandalized. And I had enough money to pay my tuition bills, thanks to gifts and part-time jobs.

While at graduate school, I became a second-generation encouragement target. "You've got the gift," Professor Jim Johnson wrote on one of my papers for his magazine-writing class. This was a man who quit writing after he became a Christian, thinking writers couldn't serve God. He became a missionary, then a pastor. Then one day Ken Taylor, who was director of a Christian publishing house, later known for his paraphrase, *The Living Bible,* urged Johnson to get back to his typewriter. He did a short story, which was soon published in a major Christian magazine. After that came more than a dozen Christian books, including the first crest of contemporary Christian fiction. As a professor, he mentored dozens of new writers, including me. Where would we both have been without an encourager?

Verbal encouragement should also embrace this truth: We employ the most powerful encouragement possible when we share appropriate passages of Scripture with people. God's Word is the Rock that makes our footsteps firm. It's the "new song" that encourages discouraged people. Scripture can reinforce our efforts to be reacher-outers and lifter-uppers. Other times it sends people on with firmer footsteps.

During that lonely year after my parents died, I read the Bible a lot, but sometimes it didn't affect me until somebody brought a truth to my attention. One day a former coworker called with a possible free-lance writing assignment. I was so grief stricken that I doubted my ability to concentrate and do an adequate job. She was adamant and finally said, "You will get through this. Remember Nehemiah 8:10: 'The joy of the Lord is your strength.'" I took on the assignment, which became the therapeutic reminder that I could still write.

As I finished my graduate studies a year and a half later, I often saw another graduating student who, like me, was experiencing difficulty finding a job. We both wondered why God was delaying answering our prayers for employment. But this friend had her feet on the Rock. One day she called to share that Rock with me. "I found just the verse for you—Hebrews 6:10," she said. "'God is not unjust; he will not forget your work and the love you have shown him as you have helped his people and continue to help them.' Jeanne, you've been faithful to the Lord. He will be faithful to you. I just know it!" I put that verse on a three-by-five card above my desk. Eventually we both found jobs, but in the meantime her warm words helped me.

A few years ago, a friend found himself in a difficult spot, sought for a position from which another friend had just been fired. I knew his gentle, peacemaker personality would bring healing to that job and situation. I didn't know how to emphasize that until some verses jumped out from my reading of Esther. I went to him and shared Esther 4:14: "Who knows but that you have come to royal position for such a time as this?" The job opening was no "royal position," but it needed God's man. He took the job and rightly earned a good reputation there.

Mouth Guards

Both my children have $4,000 smiles (and a very smiley orthodontist). The joys of braces included wearing mouth guards during active sports. I never got used to seeing them run up and down the gym or field with big yellow or blue smiles. But those pieces of plastic protected our major investment!

God's Word also offers advice for protecting our investment of verbal encouragement. The first comes out of Ephesians 4:29: "Do not let any unwholesome talk come out of your mouths, but only what is helpful for building others up according to their needs, that it may benefit those who listen." The word *unwholesome* literally means "putrid" or "rotten." Few of us enjoy being around someone with bad breath, much less a bad mouth! Instead, what we say should be edifying, timely, and Christ conveying.

Those standards helped me when I stopped to chat with a neighbor whose newly widowed sister was visiting for an extended time until her health improved. My neighbor began disparaging the sister's family for neglecting her. My mind raced. I didn't want to reinforce the criticism of people I didn't know. What could I say that would be edifying, timely, and Christ conveying? Gently I replied, "You're a very special person for this hard time of her life. I honor what you're doing."

Another mouth guard comes from the same passage, Ephesians 4:31-32: "Get rid of all bitterness, rage and anger, brawling and slander, along with every form of malice. Be kind and compassionate to one another, forgiving each other, just as in Christ God forgave you." Spiritual mouthguards are constructed of heart tissue. We can't be effective verbal encouragers with unforgiving spirits. I once worked with someone who spoke harshly and negatively to me. Even talking through the problem didn't help much. I was tempted to bite back but instead prayed that God would fill me with love for her and make my speech encouraging to her. I'm still learning that lesson as God allows other people to cross my path and "cross" me. Every time, I have to go right to the Cross.

Speaking Up

My hearing isn't what it used to be. Sometimes when I'm assaulted by the simultaneous sounds of the television, stereo, microwave, air conditioner, and vacuum cleaner, it's hard to hear the telephone ring. Take away these distractions, and I can hear very well, thank you!

I have similar challenges in speaking encouragement.

Shyness, cowardice, and pride keep me from responding when God tells me about someone who needs the healing tone of a human voice. But I've learned there's great joy in hearing and obeying the Holy Spirit's prompting.

At Jesus' transfiguration, the heavens thundered with God's great affirmation of his Son: "This is my Son, whom I love; with him I am well pleased" (2 Pet. 1:17). We, too, should seek to please our heavenly Father, even through the very words we speak to others.

Groomed to Bloom

1. When God commissioned both Isaiah and Jeremiah to ministry, he brought special attention to their mouths. Isaiah's tongue was burned with a live coal from the heavenly altar (Isa. 6:6-7). Jeremiah's mouth was touched by God (Jer. 1:9). What would God say about your tongue?
2. When Christ gasped from the cross, "Father, forgive them, for they know not what they do," he established the basis for verbal encouragement. What does that mean in your life? See Ephesians 5:1-2.
3. Read 1 Thessalonians 3:9. Who has helped you find spiritual joy? Call them up and tell them what they mean to you.
4. Looking at the section "Mouth Guards" above, review what should characterize our speech, according to Ephesians 4:29. Recall a conversation in which you might have responded differently with these guidelines.
5. Here's a wonderful prescription:
    "An anxious heart weighs a man down, but a kind word cheers him up" (Prov. 12:25).

3

Living Up to the Label

The Encouragement of Writing

I wonder which roses Shakespeare sniffed in an English country garden when he came up with these famous lines in *Romeo and Juliet:*

> What's in a name? That which we call a rose
> By any other name would smell as sweet.

I hate to disagree with the Bard, but I think there's a lot to a rose's name. Some of my favorite reading is my husband's mail-order rose catalog. If the photos with those dew-kissed colors don't leave you panting, the names and descriptions will. Why call it a "pretty red rose" when you can wax like this: "a fugitive red, maroon and scarlet . . . the kind of rose you'd send with a box of chocolates—classy, smoldering, passionate—its fiery, multiple blooms glow like coals." We don't have that particular rose in our dozen-bush collection by the driveway. But many of our plants do live up to their image-conscious names: "Pristine," "Fragrant Cloud," "Peace." Just weeks after I've pruned them to ugly thorny stumps, they explode with beauty that even gets our mailman's attention.

People aren't much different. What's written for and about them can encourage them to "bloom" more than we realize. Some of my greatest encouragement came through written means, when people cared enough to write what was on their hearts.

Many people try to dismiss themselves from the ministry of written encouragement, saying they have awful handwriting or "can't spel wurth beens." But "encouragement notes" aren't doctoral dissertations or articles you'd turn in to the local newspaper. They're simply a little bit of you on paper. Some of the "rules" of journalism, however, apply to writing encouragement. They include the ageless reporter's questions: who, what, when, where, why, and how much.

Who?

Who should write? *All of us.* We need the spirit of one of the "nobodies" of the Bible, a fellow named Tertius who's mentioned in only one verse at the tail end of Paul's masterpiece treatise to the Romans: "I, Tertius, who wrote down this letter, greet you in the Lord" (Rom. 16:22). We know little more of him than that Paul dictated the letter to him in Corinth. He was either hired help or a believer who felt his spiritual service could be his penmanship. Perhaps he knew people in Rome. More likely, while taking Paul's dictation, he was so gripped by Paul's grand spiritual message that he wanted to let the recipients know that he, too, was "in the Lord."

Tertius reminds us that we don't have to be a "somebody" to minister written encouragement. Our messages may be very simple, but words penned for God are never simplistic. Written encouragement can pack more power than verbal encouragement for two reasons. First, it's easier to face somebody on paper than in person. Even the apostle Paul, despite all his experience preaching, admitted to being "'timid' when face to face with you, but 'bold' when away" (2 Cor. 10:1). Second, what is written can encourage over and over. Whenever someone writes to encourage me, I reread that note until it's nearly memorized. Each time those words give me a boost.

Many people complain it's too hard to write. They need to meet Kenneth, an insurance investigator until a stroke at age thirty-one left him paralyzed. He can only blink and move his eyes up and down. He communicates through an alphabet board (like those used in the "Hanoi Hilton" of Vietnam times) by signaling with his eyes when a helper comes to the letter he wants. For several hours a day he "dictates" letters of encouragement that have gone out all over the world—letters that are bathed in the prayer that occupies his "locked-in" mind. At any time he may have a dozen letters "in process" and about two or three a day get mailed. Some go to people who, like him, are profoundly disabled. Others go to people in ministry. His wife remembers Kenneth writing their pastor one day: "Whatever you're praying about, the Lord wants you to do it." The next Sunday the pastor was in tears as he told Kenneth, "I can't share the details, but you don't know what your note did for me."

There are also people like Helen, who tries to write about twenty minutes a day to encourage people. One recent year, she wrote well over 800 letters. "I keep up with all the widows and widowers I know," she told me. "They are lonely people." Another friend keeps postcards in her purse so she can jot notes to people while waiting somewhere. Yet another keeps note paper near her Bible so she can share with others the verses of encouragement she discovers in her devotional time.

What?

Encouragement notes remind us of our spiritual treasure chest, "the hope to which he has called you, the riches of his glorious inheritance in the saints, and his incomparably great power for us who believe" (Eph. 1:18-19). The notes assure us that we're not alone. All the cosmic inequalities of sickness, death, disappointment, and tragedy will someday cease under the command of the King of the universe.

Until that time, we're to be at work encouraging one another, claiming the spiritual riches and hope that come
with being his children.

The Acute and Chronically Ill

When our bodies don't function right, we're especially vulnerable to discouragement. So are families of the sick. At
seven, I had rheumatic fever. For the year I was bed bound,
cards poured into our home, showing my parents how people really cared. Twenty years later, while I was a short-
term missionary, another set of cards cheered me when my
"souvenir" dysentery plunged my weight to a bony eighty-
five pounds. When a coworker delivered a stack of cards—
many of them homemade—I realized how much people
missed me and loved me. One added this note: "As I was
reading in Isaiah this morning I wanted to claim this verse
for you as we all pray for your recovery. Read Isaiah 58:11,
but don't read it in the King James!" Of course, I dis-
obeyed, and smiled about the "fat" reference when I read,
"And the LORD shall guide thee continually . . . and make
fat thy bones."

As a man named Carlton recovered from heart bypass
surgery, he was surprised and encouraged to receive cards
almost monthly from Dar, a friend from childhood who
lived across the state. Most were humorous and obviously
hand-picked to recall the "old days" when they played
baseball together. As the cards renewed their friendship,
they affirmed the value of even long-ago relationships.

The Terminally Ill

Those facing imminent death need to know they are loved
and that their lives have been worthwhile. They need to
know people are praying and be reminded of Scripture
passages of comfort and hope. When Charlie, a former
coworker from my newspaper reporter days, was dying of
cancer, I wrote how I appreciated his caring spirit when I
was new in town and lonely. I recalled how he slipped

helpful story ideas onto my desk and had his family include me for meals and hikes.

One pastor encouraged a little girl dying of cancer by writing letters—supposedly written by his horse—on big paper bags. The imaginary correspondence brightened her last painful weeks.

The Very Elderly

Mrs. Webber, in her midfifties, seemed old to me as a preschooler when my family moved to her neighborhood. She and her husband never had children but soon considered my sister and me their substitute grandchildren. After we moved away, my mother wrote her monthly to include her in "family things." After Mother died, I assumed that role. Mrs. Webber is now very old—more than 100 and living in a nursing home two states away. But her mind is sharp and my monthly letters remind her that she's not forgotten.

The Grieving

Sympathy cards encourage the bereaved even more when they contain a few personal words. When my parents died, I appreciated those who wrote something they remembered about Mom or Dad. A nurse who sent a card after my father-in-law's death shared a fun memory of this retired pastor, wobbly from Parkinson's disease, wanting to dance in the nursing home hall when he heard music! When I know only the deceased's survivors, I still try to write something positive. I wrote a friend: "Although I never knew your father, I can't help but believe that the sensitivity to people that characterizes your life was also true of his. Your daily care for others' needs is the greatest legacy you can carry on from him." Helen adds a thoughtful touch by including a couple of books of stamps with sympathy notes. "If I send money," she remarked, "it goes toward memorials. Usually, they need the stamps."

It's never too late to send a sympathy note. Four years

after their son's death, one couple was greatly encouraged by a four-page, single-spaced letter recalling their son's spiritual ministry. And don't forget notes on the anniversary of a loved one's death. A year after Doug died, I sent his widow, Shirley, a card with an aerial photo of the Columbia River. I told her it reminded me of the heavenly perspective now enjoyed by Doug, forever the fisherman, whom I also missed very much. She told me she kept it on her kitchen counter a long time.

The Timid, Lonely, Weak in Faith, or Low in Self-esteem
You never know how much an "I'm thinking of you" or "I'm praying for you" card or note can mean, nor how timely its arrival may be. Especially during difficult times in my life, I knew that people who cared enough to write also cared enough to pray. Even the stationery for our notes can communicate. One single young woman, pregnant and abandoned, was boosted when someone began sending "thinking of you" notes on cards depicting quilting, a hobby in which the young woman excelled.

The Criminally Alienated
Phyllis has a stack of manila envelopes holding her correspondence with troubled people whose stories she noticed in the newspaper. Some have been charged with crimes; others are the victims of crime. In her letters expressing her care, she reminds them that the real answer to life's problems is Jesus Christ.

Those Who Influence Our Lives
We need to take a clue from the account in Luke 17 of Jesus healing ten lepers in Samaria. Sadly, only one returned to thank Jesus for his healing. That statistic has prodded me to express gratitude to those who led and taught me, such as teachers, pastors, coworkers, and even bosses.

Several years ago, gratitude filled my heart for the pastor whose church I sporadically attended fifteen years earlier, during my senior year of college. His humility, concern for college students, and great love for Jesus later influenced me to decide to follow Christ unreservedly. Learning he now pastored in a nearby town, I wrote and thanked him, updating him on this "fruit" of his ministry. I think that letter meant a lot to him, for when I later visited his new church and introduced myself after the service, he reacted with real joy and the heartiest handshake I've ever experienced! One church secretary confided to me that her minister-boss's most sacred file was his "encouragement notes" folder. When he was low, he'd pull that out and read through it.

Missionaries

Missionaries get an armful of shots when they go overseas. But they need "booster shots" while there in the form of letters. We probably underestimate the impact of missionary "mail call." Even the apostle Paul, back when mail was barely a lick and a promise, looked forward to correspondence from his "mission fields" and supporters. At times he sent his "prayer letters" with a flesh-and-blood return envelope: "I hope in the Lord Jesus to send Timothy to you soon, that I also may be cheered when I receive news about you" (Phil. 2:19).

The phrase "news about you" is our clue that these letters don't have to be theological treatises. Helen says missionaries tell her they appreciate her newsy notes about who's getting married, had babies, or died, so there's not such an information gap when they return on furlough. They want to laugh, so go ahead and send cartoons or funny articles. Tuck in photos (those two-for-one photo deals make it so easy!). Comment on their prayer requests so they know you actually read their prayer letters. Share your own prayer needs. In God's family, we're all family.

If you've had a spiritual lesson lately, tell about it. Hearing of others' spiritual learning points often helped me in the struggles I faced. Even the greatest do. George Mueller, that great man of faith who founded orphanages in Bristol, England, in the 1800s, wrote Hudson Taylor in China: "An older brother, who has known the Lord for forty-four years, who writes this, says for your encouragement that He has never failed him. In the greatest difficulties, in the heaviest trials, in the deepest poverty and necessities, He has never failed me; but because I was enabled by His grace to trust in Him, He has always appeared for my help. I delight speaking well of His name."[1]

Those in Leadership
The pedestal of leadership is a lonely perch. Leaders hear criticism more than they do praise. This goes for those in government, education, and business. Helen wrote to encourage a Christian college president. Later she sat next to him at an alumni banquet. He told her he kept her letter of encouragement on his desk all year!

Those Who Serve Us
When was the last time you dropped your pastor a note about something from his sermon that moved you to action? Or commended the youth minister for his sensitivity to a troubled situation? Or thanked your child's Sunday school teacher? One morning when my husband was out of town, I found myself stranded in the grocery parking lot with a dead battery. Igor, the carry-out assistant, jumped my battery not once but twice with extraordinary good manners. I wrote a note of commendation to his employer, knowing that too often such good deeds go unheralded. When my children were younger, I wrote notes of appreciation to their teachers. When they became older, my children wrote their own notes at the end of the school year.

Your Own Family!
Families that drift apart are often the ones that let communication slide when members leave home. It seems that out

of sight means out of mind. One remedy could be that simple postcard, which takes five minutes to fill out and costs much less than a long-distance telephone call. Regardless of what a card says in print, it says silently, "Hey, you're missed. You're important to us. We love you." It girds up the family support system.

When?

Some people use birthdays or anniversaries as special occasions to write encouraging notes. Instead of a commercial card, they send a love letter. One young man, on his first wedding anniversary, thanked his in-laws for preparing their daughter to be his wife. He told which traits and skills he appreciated. I'm sure his stock in that family went up several points! Another person sends her annual Christmas-type greetings in November, but instead of writing a predictable list of "happenings" fills her letter with grateful thoughts of God's blessings. Then she adds a personal line telling why she's grateful for the person receiving that letter.

Most nudges to write encouragement, however, will come to us quietly from God's Spirit. We need to listen when he plants those thoughts. Too often we're like a card I saw one time in a card rack for "why I haven't written." The card said something to the effect that the sender had thought about writing three times, so the receiver now owed him three letters! Humor aside, one of the greatest tragedies of encouragement is the letter not sent.

But there are great blessings when a letter comes at exactly the right time. When a missionary friend, Helen, got word that a prayer supporter was dying, she dropped everything to write this woman of their love and appreciation for her life. It was a very inconvenient time. Helen was surrounded by packing boxes as they prepared to leave their rural Guatemalan village for the capital the next day.

But she wrote the letter and tucked it in her purse for the exhausting twelve-hour drive to the city. There, she obeyed an inner urge to take the letter to the flight counter of the airport. When the letter arrived in Oklahoma, a friend checked the woman's mailbox and took it immediately to her in the hospital. It was read to her just before she slipped into her final coma.

I can tell a similar story. My mother died just three months before my parents' thirty-eighth wedding anniversary. As the anniversary date, September 29, approached, I was halfway across the country at graduate school. But I hurt for my dad and wanted to assure him of my love on that lonely date.

I wrote neighbors, asking if they might include him for dinner that day. But I also knew something else special had to come from me. I found a card at the campus bookstore that said, "When you are alone, Jesus is there." Then, as tears streamed down my cheeks, I wrote a letter of love, affirming him as a father and as a husband who cared so diligently for my mother through her years of cancer. I mailed it so it would arrive on the anniversary day. He never mentioned the letter and ten weeks later died of a heart attack.

As I moved home to settle affairs, I dared to ask some friends if he'd mentioned such a letter. They said he had and that it meant a lot to him. I didn't realize how much, until I started sorting through piles. January passed, then February, as I went through the house. I found old birthday cards, my grade-school papers, and letters more than a decade old. But not that letter. Then in March I came to the closet where luggage was stored. I pulled out his suitcase and ran my hand through the side pockets before putting it out for a yard sale. My hand touched a piece of paper—that letter. He'd kept it with him, even taking it on his last trip just days before he died. I opened it and cried again, thankful I'd written that heart-baring letter of encouragement to him—in time.

Why?

People all around us need encouragement. Our notes can be, as Proverbs 25:25 says, "like cold water to a weary soul." One who modeled that for me was Ed, a retired coach whom I met when he was an alumni director at a Christian college.

"I like people, and I like to get in touch," he told me. "A long time ago I read about the practice of writing at least three notes a day just to encourage people. Maybe these people are going through hard times such as a death or illness. Maybe they've achieved something or been promoted. I just write them about it."

His brief, sincere notes went out to professors, students, alumni, parents, and people too old to write back ("I want to remind them that someone hasn't forgotten them," he said). He never knew how God would use his notes, though sometimes he received feedback. An alumni mom was concerned about her son, a professional athlete whom she felt could work well with young people. Ed promised to pray (another aspect of encouragement), then started watching sports pages. One day he read that an injury benched the player. Later Ed spotted pictures of him playing with residents of a farm for retarded persons and visiting children's hospitals. Ed sent those clippings to the mother with a note, "It looks as though your prayers might soon be answered."

About twenty years ago many churches took this ministry so seriously that they stuffed pew racks with "encouragement" postcards that people could fill out during service time and leave for the church to mail or deliver. One pastor told what a boost it gave him to visit somebody who was ill or hurting and hand over a fistful of cards from the congregation.[2]

How Much and Where?

It only takes a few words to encourage somebody. It doesn't

take much to fill up a postcard, but the message will speak loudly and clearly. When one pastor visited a woman dying in a nursing home, she was too ill to speak. But she gestured for her Bible and from it pulled a treasured encouragement postcard. It bore only seven words, saying she was remembered and appreciated, but it brightened her life.[3]

Some cards encouraged me several years ago when I got discouraged in a time-consuming ministry. I'd taken on our neglected church library and found myself processing hundreds of donated books in addition to mothering preschoolers. The library ministry took off—circulation rose from a handful of checkouts to nearly a hundred a week—and I was so tired I was ready to take off, too! Then a few people took the time to "postcard" their appreciation, and those few dozen words helped me hang on as librarian for several more years.

We can communicate written encouragement in ways other than cards and notes. My husband put a plate-size paper apple on a kitchen cupboard with the note, "You're the apple of my eye." One evening, exhausted from a newborn's demands, I took my baby to his crib and found this note on the pile of fresh diapers: "Zach appreciates it and so do I!" I lifted the lid to the washing machine and found this one: "Thanks for taking a load off our minds and our dirty bodies!" One man's personal treasures include a shoebox full of love messages his wife wrote on napkins she packed in his lunch. Another found "I love you" inked on his lunch box bananas. A mother found a love note on the refrigerator one morning. A father found one taped to his steering wheel saying, "Daddy, I'm praying for the man who's a problem at work." My own daughter specializes in "pillow talk" notes—and what a nice thing to find when I fall into bed! One year in February she pasted valentine message candies into a very sweet note: "Dear Mom, you are such a NICE GIRL. Since you are so nice, you should be on the WEB SITE for the best mom in the world! I'm so thankful that you LOVE ME bunches. I WILL always be very grateful for you! Congratulations on your AWESOME new book. You are so EZ 2 LOVE. LOVE YOU, Inga. P.S. HUG ME ASAP."

And don't forget banners to herald family events. The ones we tape to our living room window tell all the neighborhood that we love and care for each other. It's a real boost to drive down our street after being away for several days and see a sign that says "Welcome home!"

Sometimes "encouragement notes" can have creative "envelopes." I keep extra pie plates for delivering spontaneous "encouragement desserts" with a simple love note. After our family was in an auto accident, a friend delivered her encouragement with a box of her orchard's apples, which I could "sauce" for injured mouths. They also reminded me that I am the apple of God's eye. When one woman returned to work after a family crisis, she found on her desk a huge decorated basket filled with all types of mints, her secret passion. Attached was this note: "You're worth a mint to us!"[4]

Flowers also help say "I care" quite loudly. That's why we keep a supply of garage-sale vases in our garage to share our home-grown blooms. Even a simple bouquet from the grocery store will make a note extra special. Ida Marie, for whose paper route my family substitutes, brought me such a bouquet right after our auto accident and the diagnosis of my mother-in-law's cancer. I was operating from day to day on "autopilot." But her bouquet and a simple two-sentence note of love—from someone who's also walked alongside cancer patients—meant more than she can know.

Pressed Flowers

Sometimes I press pansy blossoms between paper towels in a thick book and later make them into stationery. It's a way to replay the beauty of my garden patch. Occasionally I forget those pressed blossoms and encounter them when I open a book for research.

Encouragement notes can be like those surprise pressed flowers. Many years ago a young woman had written to me after reading the first edition of this book. Like me, she'd gone through a broken romance and needed assurance that God was still in control. I'd forgotten about our correspondence until she wrote again after seeing my byline in a magazine. She told how she'd married a widower and inherited a lovely family. "Thank-you again for investing of yourself in my life those years ago when I was so distressed," she wrote. "I saved some of those letters with words of encouragement and Bible passages."

This time, she encouraged *me!*

Groomed to Bloom

1. Do you find it hard to express yourself? Take heart: it gets easier as you try. If you feel uninspired, browse a card shop and spend time reading unrhymed messages. Don't plagiarize, but adopt the ones that sound like you. Remember Isaiah 50:4.
2. Make writing convenient for you. Keep a supply of postcards or note paper in your Bible for people who come to mind during your devotional time. Put more in your car's glove compartment or purse. When you have a spare moment, while waiting in the car or for a meeting to start, jot a message to someone whom God puts on your heart (a favorite expression of Paul; see Phil. 1:7).
3. Tempted to "do it later"? Do it now. Don't worry about your handwriting (Paul didn't; see Gal. 6:11, which some commentators think suggests a vision problem). Type notes if it's easier; forget what people say about typed notes being "improper." If anything, they're more legible!
4. Help children develop the ministry of written encouragement. Start with thank-you notes. If they're very young, help them draw pictures of their gifts or what-

ever they're thankful for. Set the example. Leave notes on their doors or pillows. Tuck love notes in their lunch boxes. Remember Deuteronomy 6:7-8 and Psalm 102:18.

5. A reminder of this ministry:

"You show that you are a letter from Christ, the result of our ministry, written not with ink but with the Spirit of the living God" (2 Cor. 3:3).

4
Quiet! Garden at Work!

The Encouragement of Presence

Some hot summer days, when I've lost the motivation to weed and water my own yard, I collar the kids and escape to our favorite cool-off destination. For several years we've invested fifty dollars in a family season ticket to one of our area's best secrets: a scenic alpine garden on a hillside just three miles from home.

Its name is Ohme Gardens; the name is pronounced like "Oh, me!" Whenever I reach the point of sighing, "Oh me, oh my!" I know it's time to go. The kids grab a plastic bag of peanuts for the furry friends that beg at the gates. They could probably spend an hour watching those bottle-brush-tailed critters pack their cheeks fuller than the overhead luggage compartment of an airplane.

My twosome also love exploring the stone-paved trails, which lace the garden like gray yarn tangled by a cat. There's plenty to see among whispering evergreens, velvet lawns, color-blushed cliffs, and jeweled ponds. Meanwhile, Mom's off to her favorite hidden stone bench—one of dozens spaced throughout the nine acres of what used to be a private family retreat. This one overlooks the entire valley. Below me, like bugs, traffic scuttles along the north-south highway. The outdoor intercom for a fruit warehouse across the road gurgles a message. But I'm alone with my thoughts as the gardens beckon me to be still before God in a setting that reminds me of Eden. "One is nearer God's

61

heart in a garden," wrote Dorothy Gurney, "than anywhere else on earth."[1] However, just as I get near that heart, two Daniel Boone clones crawl to the edge of the cliff above me and giggle!

We have a lot of noise in our lives but too little of the sounds of silence. The same is often true of ministries of encouragement. We get so wrapped up in saying and doing that we overlook the profound importance of simply being there for somebody. We can learn much from a man with the puckery name of Onesiphorus, mentioned in only four verses of the New Testament. His name literally means "benefit-bringing" or "profit-bearing." He was the "Ohme Gardens" in Paul's life when the great apostle was literally in the pits of Rome. His life teaches these principles about the ministry of presence:

- Simply go.
- Shake self-consciousness.
- Say little.
- Share tears.
- Sustain your caring.

Simply Go

When my kids were younger, household misdemeanors often meant time-out in their rooms. However, because their rooms were stuffed with entertainment possibilities, that was no punishment until I ordered them to lie on their beds with absolutely nothing else. Sometimes, at the end of fifteen minutes, I'd find one asleep!

Those "go to your room" times were like the first of Paul's two imprisonments in Rome. The first involved a house arrest, in which he was confined with military custody but still had food, fresh air, and friends twirling in and out like a revolving door. Paul's second arrest landed him in far worse quarters. Tradition says this was the "Well-Dungeon" near the capital, a damp, cold, vaulted pit where he was chained like a criminal (2 Tim. 2:9). Humiliated, suffering physically, very alone, Paul needed an encourager. And that's when Onesiphorus came: "May the Lord show mercy to the household of Onesiphorus, because he often refreshed me and was not ashamed of my chains. On the contrary, when he was in Rome, he searched hard for me until he found me. May the Lord grant that he will find mercy from the Lord on that day! You know very well in how many ways he helped me in Ephesus" (2 Tim. 1:16-18).

It wasn't easy for Onesiphorus to "simply go" when he heard of Paul's imprisonment. He had to book passage on a ship out of Ephesus (in today's Turkey), land in Italy, then walk or catch a wagon up to Rome. Then he had to find Paul—not easy when the city had an estimated 600,000 prisoners dumped in thousands of dirty holes. It took persistent courage to go street to street, seeking out Paul. It took committed friendship to associate with a controversial prisoner. It took risking his personal safety. Can you imagine the joy that lit up that putrid pit of suffering when their eyes met?

So often we don't go to hurting people because we don't know what to say. What we fail to realize is that we don't have to talk. Usually they will talk. If they don't or can't, they just need us there. All we need to say is "I don't know what to say." Ecclesiastes 7:4 says, "The heart of the wise is in the house of mourning." Often, just being there is enough.

Shake Off Self-consciousness

A beautiful thread of Onesiphorus's character is woven with the apostle Paul's phrase, "He . . . was not ashamed of my chains." Chains limit mobility. They symbolize circumstances that others don't want to share, such as death, tragedy, poverty, crime, illness, or marital problems. Such chains may prevent the one who is hurting from seeking others for comfort and aid. But if we as "encouragers" follow the example of Onesiphorus, we won't feel self-conscious about those emotional and physical chains. We'll go because we love that hurting person and want to express Christ to him or her.

Author Jerry Bridges remembered his hesitations when a friend went through a personal tragedy. He finally called and invited the friend to lunch. For an hour as they ate together, Bridges just listened, talking only to draw his friend out. At one point the friend said, "It really meant a lot to me when you called last night." Just the prospect of someone coming had encouraged the man.[2]

There are certain types of personal overload that especially need the ministry of presence. For one, we need to spend time with those who feel dejected. After my thirteen-year-old daughter lost a close election for student body vice-president, I carved out extra time for her. We munched popcorn and watched sports on TV—it was the night her skating heroine Michelle Kwan lost a close bid for Olympic gold!—and the next day went window shopping. That weekend my daughter knew she was more important than my big to-do list because I spent extra time with her.

We need to go to those who feel rejected, such as those whose hearts are ripped apart. At twenty-five and single, I couldn't understand why my "Mr. Right" became "Mr. Gone." A mutual friend came and sat on my bed as I turned my bedspread into a swamp. But her tenderness helped me respond years later when God called me alongside some broken, betrayed single young women. Though I couldn't identify fully with their pain (I'd just had a broken heart; they had the added grief of immorality), I could still sit with them and cry and listen and pray. "Going" also applies to the great rejection of divorce. When you know both people, the issue of "taking sides" makes going especially difficult. Yet both need to know the grace of God. Both need people who "simply go" as a channel of Christ's love in this devastating human choice.

We also need to "simply go" to the sick. One busy afternoon I squeezed in a stop at the hospital where a friend had undergone major surgery. "You're the only one who came today," she said. "I needed you." I know several who've simply gone even when the hospital was a three-hour trip across the mountains—as it is for people in our valley with major illnesses needing specialists in Seattle. Lynne, for example, made those trips when Marie needed bone marrow transplants to extend her life and when teenaged Jimmy had a brain aneurysm. Then her friend Linda was diagnosed with a brain tumor.

"A few days before a serious medical test, I could tell she was really nervous," Lynne remembers. "I asked her if she'd like me to come with her. She really did." More tests and surgeries followed as this mother of four began her walk through the valley of death. Lynne's nursing background was helpful, especially as she took notes and helped Linda to articulate questions about her condition. "Sometimes all she needed was someone to sit with her," Lynne said. "I loved her so much, I wanted to do this." Being there was a simple thing, Lynne remembers, but she realized how even her presence spoke volumes after one particular test in which Linda had been anesthetized. "As we got ready to go home, she was too dizzy to put on her shoes," Lynne remembers, "so I put them on and tied them for her. She never forgot it and mentioned it several times. You would have thought I'd given her a million dollars."

We need to go to the dying. They may or may not want to talk about dying, but that doesn't mean they're denying the inevitable. They may have already settled it and just want to enjoy each day that God gives them. I remember my struggle to "simply go" to a friend with terminal cancer. We had once been in the same Bible study and had kids about the same ages, but for the most part our friendship had dwindled to "hi-and-bye" in the church foyer. Then came the news that doctors measured the rest of her life in months. Forthright about her faith, she'd already planned her funeral. Finally, I worked up the courage to call and ask when I could visit. Armed with a loaf of banana bread, I showed up after dinner feeling very awkward about my visit. "How are you feeling?" I blurted as I sat on a chair opposite the couch where she lay.

In her no-nonsense way, she replied, "Let's not talk about me. Let's talk about you." That wasn't why I "came calling"! But her reply reminded me that I needed to let her take the lead in conversation. It was more important that I come than that I know the "correct" thing to say. Her preteen daughter was banging dishes in the after-dinner cleanup, and that led our conversation to laughing over how we try to teach our children those vital homemaking survival skills. Then we talked about her favorite dog, a blue-blooded critter with a foot-long name, which starred in a television commercial. When I got ready to leave, the medical details of her illness finally entered our conversation, allowing me to pray with honesty for the future.

We need to go to those who grieve. The grieving even begins before a person dies. Lynne was still there for Linda at her deathbed, waiting and praying with the family as Linda's coma became her graduation to heaven. It wasn't easy. Three months earlier Lynne had gone through "being there" for her father's death. "But it was a great blessing for me to be a part of this hard time for them," she said. I remember the night my mother died of cancer. As we sat in the dark stillness, listening to Mom struggle to breathe, a neighbor waited in the nearby lobby, praying, just being available as we took breaks. Her presence meant so much. Thus, years later, I understood my husband's heart when he quickly changed his evening plans after answering the phone. "I'll be at the hospital awhile," he told me as I continued our kids' bedtime routine. A friend's relative was dying, and he simply went to be among them during the death vigil.

Those vigils for the grieving can also include the time

until the funeral. My father died alone of a heart attack. My sister was living on the other side of Washington state, and I was at graduate school in Chicago. I flew the next day to Seattle and my sister picked me up, then we drove thirty miles south to our parents' home to regroup for Dad's funeral. How I dreaded going into the house with the full realization that both our parents were gone. As we pulled in the driveway, we noticed a car parked in front. In minutes, we were enveloped by the arms of my mother's Uncle Bill and Aunt Mayme. Hearing of Dad's death, not knowing how they'd connect with me or my sister, they'd simply driven more than five hours from central Oregon just to be there for us. Their presence was a tremendous encouragement.

We need to go even later. Though the actual time of crisis is the most urgent time to be there for somebody, we need to remember that hurts don't disappear overnight. People who've lost a loved one appreciate those who simply come with no agenda except to be encouragers and comforters. For several months after my father-in-law died, people often asked me, "How's your mother-in-law doing?" I'd answer, "There are times when it gets lonesome. Why don't you drop by and visit her?" Those who did greatly encouraged her, affirming her as a person and upholding the memory of the one she'd loved so long.

My husband "goes" to encourage his widowed mother by getting her "going." He gets her in the car and they drive up along the Columbia River to see bald eagles or other wildlife. They come back refreshed and reconnected. Years earlier, in my own season of grieving, others did the same for me as they took me for a ride or shopping. Even though I wasn't the cheeriest conversationalist, their spending time with me helped me see how much God loved me.

Finally, we need to go for life's celebrations. We need to show up at weddings, birthdays, anniversary receptions, retirement parties, showers, concerts, recitals, games, and other events that are important to a person we care for. It's not simply for fun, it's simple affirmation that a person's life and achievements are important.

Say Little

New parents can hardly wait for their baby's first words. They listen carefully to catch those babbles that sound like *mama* or *dada*. Soon, though, those little linguistic lions drive us crazy with three other words: *No! Me! Why?* We listen a lot less! Unfortunately, when those little lions get about halfway to adulthood and can use thousands of words, we still tune them out. My daughter was dealing with an early-teen Big Issue that wasn't all that big to me. Rather than really listening to the Bigger Issue underneath the Big Issue, I launched into Parent Lecture #347. It was easier to slap on a one-size-fits-all analysis instead of really listening to my child's heart. She got my attention by rolling her eyes and moaning, "I don't need a lecture. I need you to listen!"

Too often I'm like the talkative friends of Job, the Old Testament's famous sufferer. In a breathtaking swoop of devastation, Job lost his wealth, his children, and his health. He still had his wife, but she wasn't any bluebird of cheer. She took one whiff of him, sitting in agony with ulcerating sores covering his body, and snapped, "You have rotten breath!" (Job 19:17). Job didn't need condemning words. He needed compassionate friends. For a week he had them. Three came and did the Oriental grief-thing of tearing their clothes and throwing dirt on themselves, and sat silently at his side for seven days. If they'd bitten their tongues, the book of Job would have ended after three chapters. But our Bibles have thirty-nine more chapters because these three "friends" preferred to say much and listen little. They were certain that some sin in his life caused his misery. In the middle of their accusatory preaching, Job fussed, "You are worthless physicians, all of you! If only you would be altogether silent! For you, that would be wisdom!" (Job 13:4-5).

Like Job, when people are bleeding emotionally, they don't want anybody beating on their wounds. Instead, they want someone to come alongside and just be there. One study suggested there are 700,000 ways to communicate without words. We don't just speak the message, we are the message—even as listeners. But there's a strong spiritual reason for listening. Dietrich Bonhoeffer observed that secular therapy is based on the fact that people can be helped by merely having someone listen to them seriously. "But Christians have forgotten," he added, "that the ministry of listening has been committed to them by Him who is Himself the great listener and whose work they should share. We should listen with the ears of God that we may speak the Word of God."[3]

Sometimes we need to encourage people with the truths of God's Word. Other times we just need to listen with the ears of God. Joe Bayly remembers being torn with grief after burying one of his sons. Somebody came and talked "of God's dealings, of why it happened, of hope beyond the grave. He talked constantly. He said things I knew were true. I was unmoved, except to wish he'd go away. He finally did. Another came and sat beside me. He just sat beside me for an hour and more, listened when I said something, answered briefly, prayed simply, left. I was moved. I was comforted. I hated to see him go."[4]

Author Keith Miller remembers how, after his father's funeral, one old white-haired, leather-skinned man sat all evening on the end of the couch holding his Stetson hat. Finally, when everyone else had gone, he came to Miller, looked straight at him, and said, "Son, I knew your daddy, and he was a fine man." They shook hands and the man left. Though he said little in words, his presence said much.[5]

Another woman recalled the difficult days as she cared for a sister dying of cancer. One day a friend drove seventy-five miles one way just to visit them. They took their children swimming and just spent time together. "That day was like a breath of fresh air, easing the stress I felt," she wrote.[6] That's exactly what Onesiphorus was to Paul—a breath of fresh air in that foul prison. Scripture doesn't record their conversation. Perhaps they talked about Onesiphorus's family and the church back in Ephesus. Or perhaps Onesiphorus just sat down and listened to the battle-weary apostle. Then he left to get Paul fresh food and warmer clothing, returning to sit and listen again.

Share Tears

Sometimes my young teen-age daughter doesn't know what to do with her blubbery old mom. That's especially true when this "don't-watch-TV" mom breaks down and pops in a video. This time it was *Shadowlands*, the love story of C. S. Lewis and Joy Davidman. I was determined to watch the movie intellectually, deciding where Hollywood really stretched the truth about the creator of the allegorical land of Narnia. But the gripping story of an old intellectual bachelor learning to love finally got to me. "You're not crying, are you, Mom?" Inga asked from a nearby corner where she was preoccupied. "No (sniff, sniff), why should I?" I replied. "It's just a movie!" But when the movie came to the scene after his wife's death, where Lewis and his stepson sob together in the attic, it was pull-off-the-glasses-and-grab-the-whole-box-of-tissues time.

It's okay to cry—even over sad movies. It shows we have tender hearts. Someone once said that we truly know compassion when we can taste the salt of each other's tears. When we let our own tears come, we give the other person permission to cry. I love the story told about a little girl who went to the mother of a playmate who died. When the little girl came home, her mother asked what she did. "I just climbed up on her lap and cried with her," she replied.

I read of a pastor who went to visit a couple whose teenager had been killed. He met the parents with a hug and said, "I've just come to weep with those who weep." I remembered that simple line when word came that my neighbors' brilliant, highly respected son was killed when he apparently fell asleep at the wheel. As I went to their home with a loaf of fresh-baked bread, I just said, "I've come to weep with those who weep." That's all I needed to say. The bread was put on the kitchen counter and we sat down to talk and cry.

We don't always need to know people well to share their tears. One icy winter afternoon, a friend went to the city cemetery for the graveside service of a stillborn twin. She told me later, tears gleaming in her eyes, "I didn't know them very well, but I wanted to be there for them. I was too choked up to say anything."

It is never too late for tears. I was talking with a friend about a loss in her life that happened many years before. Suddenly I felt overwhelmed and unable to hold back my tears. We weren't playing "Simon Says," but she started crying, too. In our awkwardness we couldn't find the tissue box to sop it all up. Through our tears, though, we were able to smile and appreciate the release that this tender moment had brought for both of us.

Sustain Caring

A few years ago I saw a television special on a drive-through funeral parlor. Zip, you drove up to a windowed area, viewed the deceased in his or her casket, signed the book, and zip you were out of there. I couldn't believe it! Yet that's how a lot of us treat the encouragement of presence. We hit it once, at the crisis, and then we're out of there. It's such an uncomfortable ministry that we don't like being around a hurting person very long. How wrong we are!

Twice in the passage about Onesiphorus, Paul stated his

hope that God would show mercy to Onesiphorus. The implication was not that Onesiphorus needed a special measure of grace for past sins, but that his reward would be great for his simple but personally extravagant act of going to Paul's aid. Onesiphorus's trip to Rome wasn't the first time that he reached out to Paul. "You know very well in how many ways he helped me in Ephesus," Paul wrote Timothy (1:18). For many years, Onesiphorus had simply been there for people who hurt and needed encouragement.

Those who minister with their presence sustain their caring as careful listeners even long after the crisis that brings them to the side of someone who hurts. Paul Tournier, considered one of the great people-helpers of the twentieth century, was asked one time to share his secret for counseling. He replied, "I don't know how to help people. I simply listen and love and try to provide a safe place where people can come and report on their progress without any judgment."[7]

When we say little, we must listen lots. We help people when we allow them to verbalize their feelings of loss, and we can be better listeners if we understand the emotional journey of grief. The studies of Elisabeth Kübler-Ross, on the grief emotions of the terminally ill, can also be applied to other losses. Besides death and dying, a person can grieve a lost romance, a pregnancy out of wedlock or an abortion, the birth of a handicapped child, a job loss, a business failure, a marriage failure, or a shattered dream. Each of these carries its own emotional pain and requires a time of healing.

Often the first emotion felt is denial. A person rejects the trauma and goes into shock, wanting to believe it hasn't happened while realizing it has.

Second, there's anger, blaming others or God for what has happened.

Third, guilt begins, as the grieving person internalizes anger and claims blame for what happened.

Fourth is genuine grief, often with depression and crying spells.

Finally acceptance comes and a desire to reconstruct one's life.

In all of these stages, a person needs a listener. Especially in the early stages of grief, a person may retell the details and relive the emotions many times. Sometimes the grieving person may need encouragement to express feelings. A compassionate listener can help draw out feelings by saying, "You must feel bewildered," "You're really hurting today, aren't you?" or, "I wish I could crawl inside you and bear your pain for a while."

Sometimes a nonthreatening setting can help a person talk. Some may feel comfortable on the same couch or bench. Others like to be on opposite sides of a table, with an arm's distance between them and the next person. This enables the listener to have eye contact and touch a person as appropriate. Others may open up if they go on a walk or a ride. After my mother died, my dad was most comfortable talking as I went with him on the slow walks the doctor recommended for his weak heart. We had other "heart mending" going on, that's certain!

Other people need telephone time to grieve. One woman assured a divorcing friend that she could call any time she needed to talk. Sometimes those calls came quite late at night when her pain over rejection seemed to intensify. Listeners may also need to take the initiative to phone someone when a personal visit might be difficult or intrusive. In the year after my parents died, I lived alone at their home, selling off belongings and fixing it up for sale. The loneliness sometimes overwhelmed me. Then one of my parents' older friends started calling weekly. Her first question was, "I just wondered, how are you doing?" Because she'd traveled a similar journey as a widow, she knew how much I needed an understanding listener.

Listeners are also sensitive to dates on the calendar that

might be difficult for a person in grief. Everybody thinks of Christmas or Mother's Day, but how about anniversaries of births or deaths? Exactly one year after my dad's death, I was jolted out of bed by a phone call from halfway across the country. "I know what this day is for you," came the familiar, quavery voice of a woman who'd become a surrogate grandmother to me. "I just wanted to tell you that I love you." I was touched that she remembered the date—because I did and I was hurting. As we talked, I was able to recount how much God had helped me in my first year of grieving.

Listeners are the unobtrusive caretakers in the garden of hope. When I visit Ohme Gardens and enjoy the peace, I momentarily forget the labor that goes into keeping the alpine getaway trim and refreshing. All the little patches of lawn are trimmed with push mowers. Hundreds of hours of down-on-your-knees clipping and weeding keep the ground cover controlled. It's hard, constant work. So is being there for somebody and listening. It's also hidden work. Onesiphorus rated only four verses in the Bible. But within those verses are four words to challenge all of us: "He often refreshed me."

We can encourage—even quietly.

Groomed to Bloom

1. Was there ever a time when you wished somebody had simply come to be with you? How do you identify with Psalm 142:4?
2. Recall the biography of Barnabas. What happened in Acts 9 between verses 26 and 27? Why did this take courage?
3. What is the profound lesson about tears in John 11:35, the shortest verse in the Bible?
4. Proverbs 11:25 says, "He who refreshes others will himself be refreshed." Share an incident where you've experienced this.

5. This verse reminds us of God's presence through his "quiet" comforters: "The LORD is close to the broken-hearted and saves those who are crushed in spirit" (Ps. 34:18).

5

Hugging Cacti

The Encouragement of Touch

My mother was an undaunted interior gardener. I was seven when we moved from Los Angeles to drizzly western Washington, and she immediately missed the sunshine (though none of us missed the smog). But she brought along some prickly critters to allay her homesickness. Her precious family of cacti soon lined a shelf under the west, somewhat sunny, picture window of our living room.

My favorite, a hairy specimen known as "Old Man of the Andes," just squatted there and did its regular cactus thing. But some of its cousins reacted to the new humid environment by overgrowth. Mom propped them up with spare yardsticks, but some rotted, unable to cope with the change.

I didn't really think too much of our sickly, sticky window decorations until our family acquired a cat, a rather icy-blooded Siamese named Bamboo. Most of the time the cat earned its keep blocking the furnace register, which delivered a healthy whoosh of desert air whenever room temperature dropped below 70. But when the sun dared to push apart the rain clouds and seared through our windows, Bamboo discovered the cactus shelf was a lot warmer. The cat's window-dwelling aspirations didn't last long, however. One day Bamboo reverted to amorous cat behavior and started to rub up against a thorny window-mate.

I remember Bamboo's fast departure from Cactus Corner whenever I get around somebody who's "touchy" about touch. There were times in my life when I was just as skittish as that old cat. As a young adult, still licking my wounds from a loved-and-lost episode, I redrew my "touchable" comfort zone. People found me as unhuggable as a saguaro cactus. I am thankful that the Lord softened me to give and receive the ministry of touch by teaching me these truths:

- Jesus touched as an extension of his Father.
- The Father created us to be "in-touch" people.
- Just the right touch goes a long way.
- Touch especially encourages the "untouchable."

The Touch of the Master

Above my writing corner hangs a simple portrait of a man's hands, the marks of crucifixion evident at his wrists. Next to it I posted some calligraphy of Psalm 63:3-4 that ends, "I will lift up my hands in Thy name" (NASB). That's exactly what Jesus did: he lifted up his hands on a splintered cross, in his Father's name. As I read the Gospels, I am struck by the many references to Jesus' hands. This seems especially true of Mark, long called the "servant Gospel" for its portrayal of the Savior at work. As Mark gets underway and the miracles start accumulating, so do the references to touch.

In the very first chapter, after driving out an evil spirit with a word, Jesus went to Simon's house. But the hostess, Simon's mother-in-law, was in bed with a fever. Most women have the capacity of rallying to emergencies, even when they're walking germ factories. But this lady was very, very sick. Jesus went in, simply took her hand, and helped her up. Mark 1:31 is such an understatement: "The fever left her and she began to wait on them." I wonder if, after that, she wanted to wash the hand that Jesus touched! When I was in high school, a classmate had somebody famous autograph her hand. She said she'd never, ever wash that hand—and didn't, until a hygienic mom overruled!

A few verses later, Mark tells about Jesus' coming upon a leper who begged for healing. "If you are willing," he said, "you can make me clean." Talk about begging the question! Would Jesus ever say, "No, I'm not willing to heal you"? Of course not! But this situation was more magnificent than Jesus' just healing the next person who came along. Lepers were utterly despised. Nobody dared get near them for fear of contracting one of the most dreaded diseases of the time. Laws required lepers to stay at least six feet away from people. The disease was thought so contagious that nobody would enter again a structure "contaminated" by a leper. And the leper had to announce his despised condition by calling out, "Unclean! Unclean!" to anyone approaching. But here came this leper, ravaged by a disease that deprived him of feeling touch, asking only for this Man to take away his scourge. Jesus could have healed him at the "legal" distance with a word of authority, as he had just done with the demoniac (Mark 1:25). But instead, Mark 1:41 says, "Filled with compassion, Jesus reached out his hand and touched the man." Heaven's healer knew no rules about touching.

As Jesus continued to travel, preach, and heal, word spread quickly. Everybody wanted to connect with this Man whose touch gave evidence of God. Mark 3:10 says that those with diseases kept pushing forward to touch him. In Mark 5, the synagogue ruler Jairus begged Jesus to come touch and heal his dying daughter. As the crowded street turned into a circus of the curious, another "toucher" came—a frail woman whose chronic bleeding problem left her both penniless and ceremonially "unclean." Ashamed of her condition, yet clutching a shred of faith, she stumbled forward to simply touch the edge of Jesus' cloak. While Jesus turned to grant that woman health and hope, word came of the little girl's death. But Jesus still went to her home and took her hand to lift up her body . . . to life. In Mark 6, Jesus' hands crumbled five loaves of bread and two fish, which fed thousands. In Mark 7, Jesus put his fingers into a deaf man's ears and touched the man's tongue—and the man heard and spoke. More touches: a blind man saw (8:22-25), a demon fled out of a convulsing boy (9:27), and children experienced the warmth of his lap and hugs (10:13, 16).

The touch of the Master. Jesus challenged all the cultural barriers of his day to bring healing, caring, and hope through the simple act of touching. And such is the ministry he commits to us.

Created to Be "In Touch"

The skin is the largest organ of the body, accounting for nearly a fourth of body weight. The average adult man has twenty square feet of skin. It not only "holds us together," so to speak, but it helps regulate body temperature and communicates emergency signals of pain and pressure. Most important, nerve receptors in skin endow us with the sense of touch. It's the first sense to develop in humans and usually the last lost. It participates in the full spectrum of human emotion and expression. Think of someone you love caressing your cheek. Or the security of a baby in its mother's arms. The slapping, hugging celebration of triumphant athletes. The quiet handhold of grief. Passion and compassion merge at skin level.

Only recently have scientists begun to document the importance and power of touch. Researchers have found that sensations of touch can lower heart rates and stabilize blood pressure. One university institute reported that touch helped lift depression. When depressed and adjustment-disordered children received thirty-minute back massages daily for five days of their hospitalizations, they had less depression, showed evidence of decreased stress hormones, and slept better. Touch reduced job stress for adults given fifteen-minute massages in their offices, twice a week for four weeks. Tests immediately after massages showed them more alert and able to perform better on math problems. Even though we're reluctant to touch fragile premature babies, they are positively helped by touch. Preemies given a gentle fifteen-minute massage three times a week gained weight 47 percent faster than a control group, showed better motion response, and shortened their hospital stay an average of six days.[1]

In another study, social researchers wondered why some children from one orphanage grew up to be well-adjusted adults and others didn't. Checking further, they found that the better-adjusted adults, as children, had had chronic ailments and thus needed to be picked up and comforted more often by nurses. Those who didn't have physical problems, and so didn't need as much attention, often died early or had personality problems.

Still another study claimed that men and women need eight to ten meaningful touches a day just to maintain emotional and physical health in ordinary circumstances.[2] My husband preached that message when we were first married with help from a cartoon poster he picked up somewhere and posted inside one of my kitchen cupboards. Every time I pulled down a box of cereal, I was confronted by a very unhuggable-looking creature that declared:

> Have you hugged someone today?
> I did and I feel GREAT!
> 4 hugs a day are necessary for survival
> 8 for maintenance
> 12 for growth

We definitely did a lot of growing that honeymoon year! As the years sped by, at times we lapsed into "survival," but the little hug poster continues to remind us to keep the hug therapy going. Sometimes I'll find myself hugging a family member and asking, "Are we in 'survival,' 'maintenance,' or 'growth'?"

Our culture, sadly, has been characterized as touch deprived. Families in the United States have one of the lowest rates of casual touch in the world: about two times an hour. French parents do better, touching their children about three times more often than Americans. But get ready for "growth" around Puerto Ricans. Their rate of casual touch is about 180 times an hour![3]

It isn't enough to just touch someone. That touch must come from the heart in order to touch another's heart. Combined with encouraging words or compassionate presence, touch can communicate in greater intensity than we realize. A neurosurgeon decided to see if touching his patients made much difference. For one week he spent equal time with two sets of patients, touching one group and not the other. At the end of the week, he had nurses ask the patients to estimate how much time the doctor spent with them. The ones he touched estimated he spent twice as much time with them.[4] The same impression emerged in another doctor-patient case. An old man, dying of alcoholism in a large county hospital, told nurses how he especially appreciated a certain intern assigned to his floor. The young doctor tweaked the old man's toe whenever he went by. Somebody cared enough to touch a forgotten old man.

Such studies and stories carry strong messages to those of us who claim ancestry to wooden statues. We can't afford to be stiff around hurting people. We need to ask God to break down the defenses that keep us from reaching out to care.

Just the Right Touch

There are as many ways to touch as there are flowers in the garden. And each person has a favorite way to receive this communication. My husband favors the old-fashioned bread-dough knead on his shoulders. As I fade out after three minutes, he urges, "I'll give you two hours to stop that!" The touch therapy for my mother-in-law includes doing her weekly manicure and hairdo. As I hold her hands to shape those ragged fingernails, it's our way of touching base as we talk.

But circumstances, personalities, and even culture shape just how we touch and when. One circumstance that helped me emerge from my negative attitude toward touch was working among multicultural missionaries at the headquarters of Wycliffe Bible Translators. The Latin American ties of many of its earlier workers made the *abrazo* (a big hug) the unofficial mission greeting worldwide. Your age, sex, or status in the mission leadership didn't matter. Within the mission family, you qualified for an *abrazo*. I remember one day an eighty-nine-year-old volunteer stopped an executive in the hall. "I just want to thank you for letting me work here," the elderly man said with deep meaning. They shook hands, and then the executive gave him a bigger-than-life *abrazo*. You can bet he felt appreciated!

But I learned the hard way that what's okay in one culture isn't in another. One spring my adventurous boss sent me (whose knowledge of Spanish and Hispanic culture was barely a notch above Taco Bell) to interview missionaries at a remote Indian village in southern Mexico. I noticed the Indian people greeting me with their hands extended. Wanting to be very proper, I grabbed their hands for a warm handshake. Their limp responses and strange smiles clued me in that something wasn't quite right. Then I noticed the missionary with me greeted another Indian friend by gently caressing the palm of the hand. I was enthusiastic, but she was accurate!

We don't have to go to the jungles of Mexico to encounter very different touch codes. We have it within the subcultures of our own country. Ethnic backgrounds, personality tendencies, and occupational habits all come into play. For example, think of what these labels bring to mind: Asian, Mediterranean, everybody's friend, perfectionist, drama teacher, math professor. Beyond that, each person has set certain parameters for acceptable touching resulting from family background, relationship to the toucher, and perhaps also from a bad experience involving touch. Some people also are emotionally wired such that a little touch goes a long way and sometimes the wrong way. One pastor shared his caution in this area as he remembered a woman who greeted him after the service, full of enthusiasm for his sermon. As she spoke, she caressed the top of his hand—a gesture which bothered, not encouraged, him. Definitely, there are different strokes for different folks!

When we touch the wrong way, we're like a weird plant called the *mimosa pudica* or "sensitive plant." I first encountered this novelty perennial in junior high biology. Its little fernlike branchlets droop and fold up with astonishing speed whenever they're touched. I always joked I had the touch of death with houseplants, but this one proved it. Happily, it perked up again after a few minutes. But many people "fold up" and cut you off when a compassionate touch for some reason offends them. But there's too much good from touch to back away from practicing it.

The ministry of touch has many expressions. We can pat, shake, or squeeze hands, or simply touch hand to hand. We can lightly touch arms. We can put an arm around a shoulder or a waist. We can massage a tight neck, rub a sore back, or knead a complaining muscle. And, most obviously, we can enter the wonderful world of hugs.

Hugs have many shapes and intensities. There are front hugs, sidesaddle hugs, and back hugs. Front hugs include back-slapper and back-rubber hugs. Side-hug variations pivot anywhere from the shoulder to the waist. Then you can add in the intensity of grip! All of these carry different messages. Think of how you might greet a mom or dad you dearly love and haven't seen for a while. Then think of how you should encourage somebody who's just come to you with an overwhelming personal loss, such as a death or divorce. After my parents died, a lady came to hug me. She'd known my parents somewhat but I didn't know her. She hugged me tightly and emotionally. But I wasn't comforted. We simply didn't have enough of a relationship for the type of hug she delivered. Someone else gently put her hands around my shoulders, dropped a tear, and said, "I miss your folks so much." That person comforted me.

And think of the multitude of ways we touch children. Infants get their fragile heads cradled and foreheads gently kissed. Toddlers may be toted around like a sack of potatoes, embraced like a fuzzy teddy bear, and delivered "belly blasts." Touch for older children ranges from wrestling times to those mellow sit-in-the-same chair and rock-and-talk times. We need more of the latter, minus the television. I discovered the power in rocker talks when I was still single and interacting with my nephew David. One time when I visited, he came home from kindergarten long faced and angry. He walked aimlessly through the house and avoided us when we tried to talk. Finally I settled into his father's big red velvet rocker and waved his favorite book. In a few minutes he joined me. As I wrapped my free arm around his tense little body, he started to relax. Halfway through the story I found out what bothered him at school. When I married and had my own children, I experienced the same emotional breakthroughs with touch. We had innumerable episodes of "cuddle time" in dad's rocker-recliner all wrapped up in a warm afghan. As they were touched in this "sitting-down" embrace, my children felt affirmed and comforted.

When our children become teens, with all its adolescent ups and downs, we need to keep on touching. One of my favorite cartoonists had a thought-provoking strip in which she portrayed a teenager joining her dad on the couch to watch a television show. The panels showed distance between the two as the dad looked over and thought of times when she was little and they snuggled while watching TV.

He fought the urge to put his arm around her again, thinking she'd push him away. The final panel showed the teen asking why her daddy never hugs her any more. It's better to be known as a hug-happy parent!

Can we ever hug long distance? I was frustrated in my efforts to encourage a former neighbor, who—as she entered her eighties with failing health—moved across the state to be nearer to her son. One day I went through our neighborhood with a camera and took pictures of all of us—hugging. Husbands hugged wives. Kids hugged siblings. Singles hugged pets or teddy bears. I mounted the pictures, accordion-style, and labeled the collection "Hugs from Our Street" and mailed it to her. Repeatedly in the months to follow she wrote how much she enjoyed her long-distance "hugs."

Touching the Untouchable

Touching requires a tender spirit. If you take away the letter *t* (for tenderness) in the word *touch,* you end up with *ouch.* When people are going through pain, they don't need more hurt. But sensitive touching can affirm a person in a way no other communication can. Visit some of the following "touch sites":

The Insecure

Reaching out to someone who feels he or she doesn't quite belong is like drawing a circle to include that person. I remember how one older woman wisely used touch in her ministry to singles. As a "mom-away-from-home," she expressed motherly love by lightly touching arms or squeezing shoulders. Such nonverbal attention helped the singles realize somebody cared for them and believed in them. When she hugged me, then a dateless older single, I really felt okay even though my blank social calendar implied otherwise!

The Discouraged

One day I sat at a kitchen table with a woman whose husband had been out of work for nearly a year. Her words came with difficulty and we both felt awkward as we skirted the edges of her real hurt. Gently, I put my hand over her clenched fists. My touch broke open a dam of tears, and we finally communicated. My children, now teenagers, especially need this type of encouragement as their fast-growing bodies deplete their energy and deflate their hope. When I notice the slower gait and slumped shoulders, I'll often say, "Do you need a hug?" A shrugged shoulder tells me "yes" . . . and we get into hug therapy!

Those Who Are Alone

One day I sat in on our local small claims court. The last case involved an unpaid lumber bill a builder incurred before his marriage. His distraught bride of less than a year showed up on his behalf, saying he'd disappeared. The judge commended her courage in showing up on his behalf, though the bill still needed to be paid. As I held the door for her to leave the courtroom, I couldn't mistake the agony on her face. On impulse, I asked, "Could you use a hug?" Yes, she pleaded, as she slumped to a bench. I hugged her shoulders until the plaintiffs came with an apparent desire to help her out. I'll probably never see her again, but I'm grateful I obeyed that nudge to ask permission to hug.

The Emotionally Hurting

Sometimes another's pain is too deep to talk about, and gentle touch helps them know they're not alone. Sometimes all we can do is touch and say, "I wish I could bear your hurt for a while." A friend who clerked at a local variety store went through difficult personal problems. Every time I was in that store, I'd offer her a hug and say quietly, "You're special to me." At a women's seminar, Greta was surprised to look over and see Margaret, an old friend. After a few minutes' small talk, Margaret quietly relayed her personal pain—that her husband was having an affair. As the speaker began sharing about her own failed marriage, Greta moved closer to Margaret, put her arm around her shoulder, and quietly offered some tissues for the inevitable tears. "I wanted her to feel how badly I felt for her," Greta said.

The Physically Hurting

Touching a person in physical pain can act like a culvert in diverting the emotional dimension of that pain to you. A nurse said she realized even combing a patient's hair or putting a hand on a shoulder was part of total nursing care. When a patient asked for prayer, she made sure she held a hand. Health-care professionals who touch are perceived as more committed to a patient.

Ella will never forget the touch of her doctor at the crisis point of her baby's delivery. This was her fourth pregnancy, but she had only one child at home. Her second baby, overdue six weeks and weighing eleven pounds, had been stillborn. Her third pregnancy ended in miscarriage. As Ella endured the last stages of an induced labor, calculated to prevent another tragic stillborn, a Midwestern snowstorm blew up, delaying her doctor's arrival. When the doctor finally got there, Ella's concern was overwhelming. The doctor, herself a mother, came over and put her hand on Ella's arm and said, "It sure does hurt, doesn't it?" But that simple gesture and word, Ella says, "communicated that she was with me, and she was going to go through all of it with me." The baby was born healthy. And Ella had six more children after that!

The Dying

People losing their hold on life need the life holds of those they love. They need dignity all the way to their last breath. One nursing professor remembers her early days of nursing, when her superior took her to a room where a woman was dying. "We proceeded to bathe her and change her bedding," she wrote. "Bonnie rubbed her back and powdered it, plumped her pillow and said a few words. She ministered to that patient by touch, letting her know that she was valued and loved."[5] I attempted to communicate that when strokes sent "Grandma G," an elderly woman who'd befriended me as a young Christian, to her last weeks in a nursing home. I had a new baby and couldn't visit long. But I propped my newborn just inside her bed rails so she could touch him and me at the same time. Though she couldn't talk, we communicated through contact with this new life. Years later, as my father-in-law entered his last days, family members were constantly alongside to touch him, sing to him, and remind him even as he slipped in and out of consciousness that he was indeed loved on both sides of heaven.

The Grieving

A wordless hug says more than a thousand words. These are the times when we feel as mortals the impact of the shortest verse in the Bible: "Jesus wept" (John 11:35). A pastor learned that a member had accidentally backed a tractor over his two-year-old son and killed him. As he and his wife drove to the family farm, they simply didn't know what to say. They greeted the grieving parents and embraced them. The hugs said enough; later there would be time to grapple with the implications of the heartbreaking accident.[6]

And we need to remember to touch the grieving long after a death. They continue to feel their loss, especially on birthdays, anniversaries, and holidays. On the Mother's Day after my mother's death, as a never-married thirty-two-year-old, I fought tears all through a church service commemorating motherhood. At Sunday school, a friend slid into the chair next to me and said quietly, "Today I want you to know that I care." She slipped her arm around my shoulder. It triggered the tears I needed to shed and encouraged me.

Final Touches

The ministry of touch is more than skin to skin. It's a symbol of God's creative power, the Hand that created the stars, the planets, the waters, the lands, and all that lives and moves upon the earth. Michelangelo interpreted this so poignantly when he painted the creation with a focus on the Creator's finger imparting life to the first created being, Adam. It's also a symbol of the redemption, something I think about every time I look up from my computer and see the painting of Jesus' hands. Callused from a carpenter's life, those God-hands healed people, raised the dead, blessed children, and multiplied fish and bread. Most important, those hands hold my name. An old hymn by Charles Wesley reminds me:

> Before the throne my Surety stands,
> My name is written on His hands.

When those same hands accepted the nails of Roman executioners, they gave me the mandate to reach out and touch people—for him.

Groomed to Bloom

1. Several years ago a popular religious art piece showed a child hugging the palm of a giant hand. The image recalled Isaiah 49:15-16, which perhaps referred to an ancient Jewish custom of puncturing a representation of Jerusalem's walls and temple on one's hands. Look up this verse and share how it comforts.
2. What was Jesus' last healing act before his crucifixion? Read Luke 22:49-51. What enemy have you been reluctant to touch? Corrie ten Boom told of her struggle,

years after freedom, to return the handshake of a person who identified himself as one of her former prison camp guards. When she extended her hand, the hurt melted away as God's love flowed through. How can Ephesians 4:32 help you?

3. One of the Bible's most famous hugs is that of the prodigal son and his father (Luke 15:11-32). What truth of unconditional love from this story could you apply to your life?

4. God's love is often expressed through the visual agent of hands. Read Psalm 138:6-8. What do the different aspects of hands express in these verses? Which encourage you?

5. Knowing we are special to God helps us see his hand of love when life seems out of control. This affirming verse will remind you to reach out to others on the Lord's behalf: "You hem me in—behind and before; you have laid your hand upon me" (Ps. 139:5).

GRANT REFORMED
CHURCH LIBRARY

6

Trumpet Flower Time

The Encouragement of Prayer

Just about every little girl has her royal dreams. I was no exception, imagining myself crowned and enthroned amidst hundreds of brilliant yellow daffodils. You have to be a native of western Washington's Puyallup Valley to find the romance in that! But I grew up with the dream of little Puyallup girls: being chosen from all the valley's high school senior girls to represent the annual Daffodil Festival as its queen. Yes, I even designed my own crown from cardboard my mom tossed out. And I practiced the "royal wave" in front of my bedroom mirror—with the door closed, of course!

My senior year came, and I wasn't even nominated for Daffodil Queen. One of my grade school buddies made the cut to the final selection of "princesses"—she of childhood buck teeth and thick glasses who became a beauty through braces and contact lenses. Through her we learned that all the trips and speeches involved in festival promotion weren't any bed of, uh, daffodils.

Though I missed my chance at the crown, I still do a royal job of promoting daffodils. Each spring, I can hardly wait for those brilliant yellow trumpets with their waxy texture and pungent fragrance. I can identify with William Wordsworth's ecstasy as he stumbled upon a crowd of golden daffodils: "Beside the lake, beneath the trees / Fluttering and dancing in the breeze."

Funny thing about daffodils. They start off truly ugly. The bulbs planted in the fall look like scorched turnips. But in God's time, they emerge as reflections of his glory. That's so much like prayer. I pray using plain, turniplike words to address the Sovereign of the universe. But when they reach his throne, they become a glorious bouquet. He is pleased to pay attention to this prayer gift. Then he redelivers these blooms as encouragement to the people for whom I've interceded.

I have much yet to learn about the mystery and privilege of prayer. But I know it's not an optional part of our spiritual ministries. "Intercessory prayer," observed the classic devotional writer Oswald Chambers, "is part of the sovereign purpose of God. If there were no saints praying for us, our lives would be infinitely worse than they are; consequently the responsibility of those who never intercede and who are withholding blessing from our lives is truly appalling."[1]

One who models biblical intercession is an almost anonymous man named Epaphras. His life speeds past us in four quick verses of the New Testament. But we see enough of his character to discover these simple but profound "abilities" necessary for the encouragement ministry of prayer:

- Vulner-ability
- Depend-ability
- Defend-ability
- Account-ability

Vulnerable to Others' Needs

To be vulnerable literally means to be capable of being wounded. In the spiritual realm, it means allowing the needs and hurts of other people to become part of our lives. We're vulnerable when we don't wait for people to ask us to pray. We pray as naturally as breathing.

As we consider the full stage on which Epaphras played a

part, we'll see how he illustrated this "ability." Scholars believe that Epaphras founded the church of Colossae in Asia Minor. Paul hadn't gone there; in Colossians 2:1 the great apostle referred to the Colossians and Laodiceans as those who had not yet met him personally. But he had referred to Epaphras as "a faithful minister of Christ on our behalf." Paul also called the man "our dear fellow servant" (Col. 1:7) and "my fellow prisoner in Christ Jesus" (Philem. 23). Little more is known other than that he traveled well over seven hundred arduous miles from his home in today's Turkey to see Paul, a prisoner under house arrest in Rome about A.D. 60.

Epaphras encouraged Paul with reports that his home church was growing in faith, hope, and love (Col. 1:4-5, 8). But he also reported its problems. Colossians 2 indicates the young church had accepted some heresies, including the worship of angels and a strict observance of Jewish ceremonies. These had the effect of making Christ merely a part of the church system instead of its divine focus. Epaphras could have passed off these problems as the concern of others. But he felt keen responsibility for the needs of his fellow believers. That context helps explain Paul's note at the end of Colossians: "Epaphras, who is one of you and a servant of Christ Jesus, sends greetings. He is always wrestling in prayer for you, that you may stand firm in all the will of God, mature and fully assured" (4:12).

Vulnerability in prayer comes, first of all, through our mutual love of Jesus Christ. And then, because we belong to Jesus Christ, we serve one another. As "one of you," Epaphras had opened his heart to the needs and hurts of his brethren in Christ. As "a servant of Christ Jesus," he looked after others' needs above his own. There's a lot of truth in the witty remark attributed to Ben Franklin: "The person who is wrapped up in himself makes a very small package." When we focus inward, we get cross-eyed. But when we focus Christ-ward, we see needs all around us and want to pray about them.

Vulnerable prayer-encouragers take the initiative to pray. Two friends, one of them a prominent businessman, met for lunch. As they talked, the businessman began revealing his physical and emotional exhaustion over too much responsibility, losses, and unfaithful personnel. The other man first thought of leaving his wealthy friend alone with his problems. Then he remembered Scripture's command to help his friend bear that burden (Gal. 6:2). After lunch, alone in the businessman's office, he suggested they have prayer.

"While I was talking to the Lord on behalf of both of us," he said, "this man began to sob. I looked up while praying. Tears were streaming down his face, and he was wiping them away with his big, rugged hands. At the conclusion he said to me: 'Bob, thanks a million. I don't ever remember anyone coming to my office and taking the time to pray with me and for me. This perhaps has been one of the greatest days of my life.'"[2]

I experienced similar encouragement when my mother-in-law was diagnosed with cancer and I became her "wheels" and companion for doctor appointments. Many in our church family told us they were praying for her, but I got a little more insight into the special nature of vulnerability one morning near the end of her five weeks of daily radiation treatments. One couple in the oncology waiting room had just started the husband's treatments for prostate cancer. They seemed to have a special confidence in the midst of this frustrating disease, and as we chatted I learned they were Christians. As I shared our story, the wife quickly said, "We pray every morning. We love to pray for people. We'll put you on our prayer list." She also asked for a picture of our family as a reminder to pray, and several weeks later I got a letter from her, confirming that they indeed were praying for my mother-in-law and my family. Was I encouraged? You know I was!

My friend Cecilia knows how vulnerability changed her life when muscular dystrophy took away her marriage, her mobility, and her hope for life. She was forty-seven and had to move home to be cared for by her parents. Then an old friend, Mary Lou, who'd also known the pain of divorce, came into Cecilia's life and started praying for her. "Whenever she called or visited," Cecilia recalls, "she seemed to sense what my greatest need that day was. God's love seemed to come out of every pore of her body." The love Mary Lou expressed in prayer nudged Cecilia toward turning her "churchianity" into a personal faith in a God who really cared about her difficult situation.

I saw vulnerability when a special speaker came to our church. I sought him out to greet him because I'd learned we once attended the same Bible college. After we finished talking about those roots and our present ministries, I was ready to conclude with the usual "good to meet you." He surprised me by saying: "How can I pray for you?"

This is also a spiritual quality we can nurture in our children. For many years I suffered from frog-stranglin' headaches. I didn't realize how much they affected my family until one day I overheard my children, then preschoolers, playing "house." "I'll be the mommy and you be the daddy," Inga ordered Zach, "and I have a headache so leave me alone!" For the most part, my headaches were an inconvenience to their play wants. When Mom had to go to bed in a dark room, we couldn't go to the library for story time and dinner would probably be fast food (which wasn't all that tragic for them!). But as they grew older, they became more sensitive to my physical and emotional pain. They understood that I didn't want to lose a day to headaches and that I wanted to be there for them. I wanted to be the mom that Christ intended for me to be. I realized my children were really caring for me and not just grieving the absence of their playmate, when I woke up to find a child by my bed saying quietly, "I'm praying for you, Mom." Another time I rolled over to jam my head in a pillow and noticed a hand-made get-well card with the same message. They hurt with me—and told the Lord. Their "vulner" soon helped me feel "able."

Dependable to Keep a Promise

Three little words provide the second clue to a prayer-encourager's character: "He is always." Dependable prayer-encouragers don't pass off prayer needs with a wimpy, "I'll be prayin' for ya." They often pull that person aside and pray right on the spot. They most likely write a reminder note to pray or add the request to a small prayer notebook or page in their daily planner. They may even write time-related requests ("Jim's job interview," "Mary's surgery," "The Smiths—court date") right on the family calendar so they don't miss the reminder to pray. We're creatures prone to forget; there's no dishonor in keeping lists. In fact, it reveals our compassion and sense of responsibility in this grand job of praying.

I was convicted in this area after reading the biography of martyred missionary Jim Elliot. When searchers found his body in that Ecuadorian river, speared by the tribesmen he and his colleagues tried to contact, they also found his black, loose-leaf prayer notebook. Started during college, it held the names of hundreds for whom he'd prayed. A few years after reading that, I met another praying saint. She lived in a little apartment near the church, and her enthusiasm for life masked her physical fragility. One Sunday morning a friend found her sitting up in bed, dead. In her lap was her prayer list. What a way to go!

The marching orders for encouragement prayers come right out of Ephesians 6:18: "Be alert and always keep on praying for all the saints." The term "be alert" comes from a word suggesting sleeplessness and watchfulness. Think of parents waiting for their daughter to come home from her first date—or her twentieth—and it's way past curfew! When you commit to dependability, you commit to following through.

Several years ago, as I began speaking at a retreat in a small farming community, the ladies wheeled in someone very special. I was immediately struck by the beautiful spirit evident in the face of this mother, who was severely disabled with multiple sclerosis. I learned later how several women came to her home every Wednesday night just to pray for her and her family. Her husband had a standing invitation with another man at the local doughnut shop, and her children were at Christian clubs, so the women were alone to intercede for her in her pain. The love that flowed dependably each Wednesday night helped her endure another helpless week in her wheelchair as she waited for heaven.

Too often, though, we're like Jesus' disciples in the Garden of Gethsemane. On that awful night before his crucifixion, Jesus singled out Peter, James, and John to stay close while he prayed. "Remain here and keep watch," he requested of them (Mark 14:34, NASB), and then he went a stone's throw away for the most excruciating praying he'd ever done. Depending on how much practice you've had in the batting cage and the size of the stone, a stone's throw isn't far. Yet the disciples acted like tired old dads in their recliners after dinner. When they had the privilege of talking to God the Father on behalf of God the Son, they slipped into Snoozeland. It's too bad our Bibles don't have stereo speakers, for we need to hear the sadness in Jesus' voice as he returned and woke Peter by asking, "Are you asleep? Could you not keep watch for one hour?"

Ready to Defend

Defendability is the dimension expressed in the next phrase about Epaphras's ministry: "wrestling in prayer for you" (Col. 4:12). The Bible has several famous wrestlers. The twins Jacob and Esau wrestled inside their hapless mother, Rebekah, before they were born (Gen. 25:22). They were so busy kicking and grabbing that she probably felt she was giving birth to two bombs, not two babies. I can understand that. Both my kids practiced prenatal tumbling and swan dives. I'm not surprised that one night I dreamed I was giving birth to a frog! Then Jacob, the heel grabber, as a grown man had a divine wrestling match that left him limp (Gen. 32:24). David wrestled bears and lions (1 Sam. 17:34-35). One of his mighty men, Benaiah, wrestled a lion down in a snowy pit (2 Sam. 23:20).

But the word for "wrestled" in Colossians is very special. The original Greek word there is *agonizomai*. Our English word *agonize* comes from the same root, but the Greek word has more muscle to it. In Luke 13:24 it's used to describe making every effort to get through the narrow door to redemption. When I was a skinny little kid, I enjoyed playing hide-and-seek and hiding under my low-slung bed. Then I got bigger and just about smashed my body to the point of needing first aid trying to cram under that bed. I truly wrestled to get the fatter parts of me under the frame. First Corinthians 9:25 uses the same basic word to describe the strict training for star athletes. Paul claimed the spiritual version of this disciplined, sweaty effort on behalf of new believers: "To this end I labor, struggling with all his [Jesus'] energy" (Col. 1:29).

The prayer-encourager who shows defendability prays in real earnestness, knowing the wrestling takes place in enemy territory. In Ephesians 6:12, Paul reminded us that "we wrestle not against flesh and blood, but against principalities, against powers, against the rulers of the darkness of this world, against spiritual wickedness in high places" (KJV). We live amidst an invisible spiritual war. The enemy's bombs and tanks have big names such as "immorality," "deceit," "loss," and "greed." He's also planted land mines with tags like "discouragement" and "discontent." Yet prayer can defuse these weapons.

Ironically, those with the strongest prayer muscles are often those who are the weakest physically. Remember Kenneth, the stroke victim we met in chapter 3? His mind works but he can move nothing of his body except his eyes. In addition to writing letters, he prays. "One thing Kenneth has is time," his wife says. "After he'd been paralyzed about six years, he went to a men's meeting where they were challenged to accept whatever ministry God had for them. Kenneth had his dad raise his hand for him. He felt God's ministry for him was prayer. The leaders of two Christian organizations now send Kenneth their ministry calendars so he can pray. One told us how many times he'd sensed Kenneth's prayer coverage."

My friend Cecilia, confined to her motorized wheelchair as a result of muscular dystrophy, is another who is often asked to pray for others. "God is teaching me to live with a sense of prayer all day," she says. "Even when I'm driving my wheelchair somewhere, I'll find myself talking to God. People whizzing by me on the street may wonder what's going on! But as this wheelchair forces me to travel much more slowly through life, I'm learning to be more in touch with God." Cecilia got her first lessons in "battlefront" prayers as a new Christian when she partnered with two other women in her church for a year and a half to pray for their families, church, community, state, and nation. As her prayer life has deepened, she's learned how God can intercept the enemy of discouragement. At one point her daughter was struggling financially. "I have no money, either," Cecilia told her, "but I will pray for you." The next day at work, someone handed the daughter an envelope with $100 in it. Another time Cecilia was discouraged. She'd lost the caregivers she needs for dressing and hygiene. At 10 A.M. her friends went to prayer; by 4 P.M. she had two more caregivers lined up, including one to put her to bed that night.

Sometimes the enemy also attacks the person who would pray. When a friend phoned and talked on and on about her depression, work conflicts, and physical problems, I sensed all were connected in a spiritual battle she was trying to fight alone. After twenty minutes, my ear was hot and I'd twirled the phone cord in and out of my fingers umpteen times. Then I felt a prod from the Holy Spirit, something on the order of, "Jeanne, your friend needs someone to part the clouds and show her me." Her battle involved spiritual forces; my battle was reluctance to join in the fray through prayer. Then God dropped this message in my heart: "Pray with her!" Over the phone? I complained. "Why not?" he answered.

As my friend stopped to catch her breath, I said, "Sue, I don't know what God's answer is for all this. But I want you to know that I care. Before I hang up, let's pray about it." "Would you?" she asked. I prayed for God's peace in her life, asking him to alleviate her pain if possible, to show both of us the reason, and to teach both of us acceptance. When I finished, I heard some sniffling. "Thanks," she said, "I needed that. It means so much that you would pray. I know I need to change my perspective."

Sometimes God's Spirit nudges us to pray fervently for battles we don't learn about fully until later. Whenever I wake up in the middle of the night, I often wonder for whom God wants me to pray. That's because I've heard many stories of missionaries facing danger at the precise time that a prayer warrior had a burden to pray for them. God works that way on the home turf, too. One wintry morning Cindy felt led to pray for a Christian friend who would be coming home soon from a vacation. Cindy didn't know it, but that very morning the friend and her husband were driving across a snowy mountain pass in extremely hazardous conditions. Someone cut in front of them, and then an avalanche slammed down the mountainside, entirely burying the car ahead and partially burying theirs. The timing of Cindy's prayer was no coincidence in God's eyes.

Accountable Both Ways

Accountability means that a prayer-encourager watches for answers. In addition, the person prayed for reports back to the pray-er. I know how special I feel when people offer to pray for me. I feel doubly special when they check back later to see how God answered a need. It doesn't take much—a note, a phone call, or pulling somebody aside in the hall at church. But it's like tying the bow on top of the package.

The last mention of Epaphras in Scripture, in Philemon 23, indicates he was one of those "checker-backers." In that letter to a church leader regarding a returning slave, Paul makes a quick reference to the much-traveled prayer warrior: "Epaphras, my fellow prisoner in Christ Jesus, sends you greetings." The man who entered biblical history as Paul's "dear fellow servant" (Col. 1:7) had a new title as a "fellow prisoner." Some commentators raise the possibility that he, too, had been arrested and detained. Whether he had or not, he continued to keep the Colossians' needs on his prayer accounts. Maybe this was a case of absence making the heart grow fonder.

It's easier to pray for people you see regularly and to check up on them than those at a distance. A former roommate modeled such disciplined praying for me. After she married, we still met weekly to study Proverbs and touch base on each other's lives. We each kept a small three-ring notebook for our Bible study notes, with a couple of blank sheets to mark each other's prayer needs. The left-hand column of those pages was the "date requested" and the right-hand side, "God's answer." It was easy to mark off the requests that had dates connected to them, like an upcoming ministry or deadline. Others, such as submitting to authority or developing a quieter spirit before God, were harder to measure. But because we had admitted those needs to each other, we were more sensitive to how God was changing us through daily choices. At the end of the year, when we looked over our lists to review our prayer-and-study partnership, we saw how God had honored our accountability to each other with a perceptibly deeper walk with Jesus.

At the same time, I had another, older, prayer partner— by mail. This retired nurse had entered my life more than five years earlier when I was a young newspaper reporter in her town. She'd taken me into her heart as both a surrogate daughter and a new Christian. Plagued by insomnia, she used her wakeful nights to pray. She'd write and ask me my needs and write again asking how those situations were doing since she'd started praying.

Those on spiritual battlefields—including pastors, missionaries, and parachurch workers—say accountability is the difference between thinking people are praying and experiencing the reality of it. "One lady told me she prays for me every morning," a busy pastor related. "That registers, especially when I have a day when things aren't going as well. Knowing she has prayed encourages me." I also experience that as a Christian writer and speaker. As I go about what can be a lonely and frustrating task, I am grateful that certain people have committed to pray a particular project to completion. I'm grateful for Marie and her adult daughter, Karen. "I love to pray for you," Karen has told me many times, a statement that humbles me because Karen is mentally challenged. Then there's Dagmar, who started corresponding with me after I spoke at a women's retreat she attended. Years later she was on a trip and stopped by my home with a lace-decorated fabric heart, "to remind you that you're in my heart and I pray for you." I have that hung by my bed. And as you read this chapter, months and years after it was written, you need to know that today, as I struggled to write and rewrite, the letter carrier brought a note from another prayer-encourager, Jan. She quoted Habakkuk 2:2: "Write the vision and make it plain . . . that he may run that readeth it" (KJV). I feel ably defended by these vulnerable people who are dependable and accountable.

The Total Prayer

Sometimes all "abilities" of prayer—vulnerability, dependability, defendability, and accountability—merge in such a way that they're a tightly wound cord. God may not only make us aware of a need but get us off our knees and off to the need. One Christian couple started giving up on their marriage. Despite counseling, they talked about divorce. Many of their friends felt especially concerned about their situation because their breakup would scar their children, have an impact on many ministries, and be a smudge on the name of Christ among the nonbelievers they knew.

In past years, this family had depended on others for practical help in tough spots. Now, they needed the dependability of caring people to pray—really pray. One friend said the crisis loomed so big in her heart that she was on her knees several times a day for this couple and the spiritual warfare involved. The need for defendability became more critical as the wife left town for a few days to think through her decision. During that time, some friends took meals to the family to remind the distraught father and children that they could depend on friends to pray. This couple stayed together, and several friends are still accountable to pray for continued mending of the marriage.

"Being loved is a matter of the heart, and so is prayer," wrote Rosalind Rinker, whose books on prayer thirty years ago reawakened that passion in many hearts. "Prayer is the language of the heart. Both involve giving-receiving relationships. Deny the heart either of these expressions, and it can soon become like a parched, neglected garden—no flowers, only dry dead memories—and desperately in need of spiritual healing."[3]

If we don't pray, it really matters. Hurting people will wither, like daffodils after their few weeks on display. But how grateful we can be that people aren't flowers. We were created for eternity, and the flowers we plant in heaven through prayer will bloom forever.

Groomed to Bloom

1. Expand your vision of how to pray for somebody by

personalizing Ephesians 3:14-21. Which of these petitions could you pray for someone? Which do you need prayed for yourself?

2. Some of the Bible's most famous "prayer partners" are described in Daniel 1—2. As you read the text, take note of Daniel 2:17-19. Do you think that experience strengthened both their faith and friendship?

3. First Timothy 2:1 suggests an often overlooked dimension of prayer. The last word in the list, *thanksgiving*, comes from a Greek word that literally means "grateful acknowledgment of God's mercies." Have you recently prayed thanksgivings for someone's life and ministry? Take some clues from the apostle Paul (Eph. 1:16; Phil. 1:3; Col. 1:3; 2 Tim. 1:3; Philem. 4). Then translate your prayer onto paper and write your thanks to that person.

4. The Lord Jesus embodied all the "abilities" of prayer. Decide which these represent: Hebrews 2:18; Romans 8:34; Hebrews 7:25; Luke 22:31; John 17:19.

5. Consider this verse, which expresses the teamwork of prayer: "On him we have set our hope that he will continue to deliver us, as you help us by your prayers" (2 Cor. 1:10b-11).

7
Anything Grows

The Encouragement of Hospitality

Welcome to our backyard, where anything grows—has, does, and will. Before I threw in the trowel on big-time gardening, its anemic soil hosted equally anemic carrots, lettuce, beans, corn, and squash. For many years I also kept a compost pile. The local slugs and field mice adored it. My children bragged on it. Visiting playmates getting the grand house tour ("This is the bathroom, if you need it," "This is my Barbie corner") also got to inspect our compost corner.

Then one year I abandoned my calling to be a farmer, raked the plot smooth, and threw grass seed at it. The local farmer's market promised to sell me stuff cheaper than my investment in water, peat, fertilizer, bug stuff, tools, and—most important—down-on-my-knees weeding time. At minimum wage, that garden was a pricey baby. It seemed, sometimes, that we'd planted thistle and dandelions instead of the civilized stuff. The official garden hardly grew, but weeds would bump another inch out of the ground if I even barely smiled at them.

I still "farm"—but vicariously through those home-and-garden magazines that entice me in the waiting room at the doctor's office. What hospitality I could offer "if only . . . ." By the time I've mentally remodeled the house and planted a replica of Vancouver's picture-perfect Butchart Gardens in the backyard, the nurse does a reality check and hustles me to the scale. And then it hits me: just as I have to live with the body I have (improving it where I can), God wants me to practice hospitality with the home he provides. The Bible doesn't describe hospitality with hype over folding napkins into swans or forcing jonquils in pebbles. Instead, it brings us to the very essentials of this God-ordained ministry of encouragement:

- Hospitality risks opening its guest book.
- Hospitality asks us to share only what we have.
- Hospitality lets the Lord bless the occasion.
- Hospitality doesn't seek thank-yous.

The Open Guest Book

The Bible's Halls of Hospitality are hung with many cameos of people who generously opened their homes. Sarah, laughing to herself, patted bread cakes for three mysterious visitors who announced that this wizened old lady would bear a baby (Gen. 18). Jethro took in a lonely vagabond named Moses and gained a famous son-in-law (Exod. 2:20). An angel turned down Manoah's generous offer of dinner but left him with an amazing prophecy of a son to be named Samson (Judg. 13). Abigail, apologizing for her husband's foolishness, invited David to a stadium-size picnic (1 Sam. 25). A widow at Zarephath shared with Elijah what she thought was their last meal, but they ate for years more (1 Kings 17). A Shunammite woman turned a rooftop corner into a haven for another prophet, Elisha (2 Kings 4). Job boasted of being hospitable (Job 31:32). Jesus was welcomed at several homes. Acts records how Paul enjoyed hospitality offered by Lydia and a jailer in Philippi, Jason in Thessalonica, Aquila and Priscilla in Corinth, and Philip in Caesarea.

But one of the greatest lessons on hospitality comes from the only miracle recorded in all four Gospels. Once upon a time, I thought feeding the five thousand was what the college chow hall did three times a day. I've since come to love the many truths in this story of God's generous provision.

Jesus and his disciples were by the Sea of Galilee when they got word that Herod, trapped in a frivolous promise, had ordered John the Baptist beheaded. Jesus grieved the death of his cousin, friend, and supporter. He also knew it would be safer to move away from Herod's territory. Thus they sailed across the sea to a lonely spot near Bethsaida, on the north side of the Sea of Galilee.

But their little boat was as obvious as the Goodyear blimp. Eager to hear him teach and see him heal more of the sick, crowds scrambled along the shore to their landing spot. Now some of these people were a walk of two hours or more from home, and this was desolate country. It had no Tiberias Travelodge or Bethsaida Burgers. Worse, tired and hungry people tend to become unfriendly people— and they vastly outnumbered Jesus' crew. When Jesus asked Philip where they would get food to feed everybody, he replied with an engineer's precision: "Two hundred denarii—what a man might earn if he worked for eight months—wouldn't even begin to feed all these."

Many of us share Philip's hang-ups about "enough," thinking our guests need a lake-view cottage and fresh strawberries for breakfast. But that's not the biblical view. The Greek word for hospitality, *philoxenia,* literally means "brotherly love of strangers."[1] We take people—even people we don't know—where they are, and they take us where we are.

What a ride that sometimes can be! Just talk to my friend Verna. Her former job as a church secretary included rounding up meals and housing for special guests. Tired of asking and getting turned down, she resigned herself to providing lunch and a place for the guest speaker to rest one afternoon. The speaker's name was Mr. Kerr, and Verna, a down-to-earth type, didn't give his name a second thought. That morning in staff meeting, she realized that

"Mr. Kerr" was Graham Kerr, internationally famous as "The Galloping Gourmet" and also a spokesman for Youth with a Mission (YWAM) ministries.

"I experienced the deepest sinking feeling!" Verna admits. It was too late to back out, and thus she took the famous chef home for a quick lunch. "I started pulling stuff out of the refrigerator and suggested he make the salad," she remembers. "It was a real education for me. I had the wrong tomatoes. I didn't know about spicing the salad up with basil. But that lunch was such a special time. He was easy to entertain and so gracious. He actually said it was refreshing to meet somebody who didn't know of him! I had to go back to work while he rested, and when I came home again, my kitchen was the cleanest it had ever been. My guest had been busy. Though I was terribly embarrassed at first, it was a highlight for me."

Verna says the incident held a deeper lesson, as if the Lord were asking her, "Verna, if I were coming for lunch, would you be ready?"

Many times Verna and her husband, Tom, *were* ready as they raised their family of four children in a modest house on a modest income. They sectioned off their basement for college students to room and board. They took in foster children, welcomed Japanese exchange students, and even sponsored two Polish men and a Romanian couple seeking a new start in America. There were often extra plates at the big table that nearly filled up their dining space.

"Having all these guests helped my children interact with people from a lot of different backgrounds," Verna says. "They became more sensitive to other's needs."

The demands of extra people in the house stretched Verna as she also held a job outside the home, "but those years were the highlights of my life," she said. "My faith was really tested when I took our immigrants around for job interviews or to stand in welfare lines. I saw a lot of the negatives of life, but I also saw God work in big ways. And the people who stayed with us definitely were exposed to our faith in a God who supplies!"

Sharing What We Have

Philip didn't think the crowd could be fed. But Andrew presented a little boy willing to donate his entire lunch bag: five barley loaves and two fishes. I can imagine Philip thinking, "Why, we'd need fifty bakeries and two Moby Dicks to fill up this bunch!" The Gospels say there were five thousand, but Jewish historians traditionally counted only the men present. Adding in women and children could possibly swell the number to ten thousand.

Jesus simply replied, "Order the people to sit down." Like a human garden, the weary thousands reclined in orderly rows on the soft springtime grass. Then Jesus asked for extra baskets—an easy request since many used them for luggage. Tenderly reaching into the boy's bag, he took the flat, thumb-wide barley loaves (considered so lowly by Jews that adulteresses used them for temple offerings) and dried opsarion, a common fish of the lake. As Jesus broke the bread and fish into twelve baskets, which eventually fed ten thousand, his disciples' eyes must have widened several centimeters.

Like the disciples, we may think our resources too limited or humble. But humble pie tastes great! Easter, known for her hospitality, loved to fill her table with fare from her own garden, cooked down-home Arkansas style. A missionary friend says her best furlough hospitality took place at a table covered with oil cloth and stacked with the simplest foods.

Sleeping arrangements need not be motel-perfect either. The "guest room" in our small tract home is also the pantry, library, sewing corner, Barbie-ville, TV room, office, and recording studio—all in the space of a former one-car garage. We used to have an old brown plaid sofa-bed whose mattress had the geographic features of the Dakota Badlands. It opened up right over the fireplace hearth. Guests now get the blow-up mattress on the least-crowded half of the room. Yet this junky, crowded room has hosted many guests, some in difficult life transitions. So did the kids' rooms, when they offered visitors their own, more comfortable beds and slept on the floor.

Marty and Jinny, two single women I met when they lived in the Chicago area, deliberately shared a house bigger than they needed so they could minister through hospitality. Several times they brought me home for the day or the night, sensing I needed the change to help me regain equilibrium in the months after my parents died. As I snuggled down in a spare bed, grateful for their bright conversations and simple food from their big garden, I thanked God that they didn't let their marital status bar them from reaching out. I learned how dozens of foreign students from a nearby community college also found their home a haven. So had friends of friends, strangers recommended to them, missionary families needing recovery time after surgery . . . and on and on.

"I enjoy people," Jinny told me. "I think that too many people are embarrassed to have others in if their house isn't exactly what it should be. If we used that as an excuse we wouldn't have anybody in. Our place isn't fancy. We have a lot of second-hand furniture. But we share what we have, and that's what the Lord wants."

Tom and Phyllis share an "empty nest." Active and well known in Washington state rodeo circles, they express their faith in showing hospitality to hurting people. When one young man, whose mother Phyllis had known, got out of jail, they decided to help him get a fresh start. Tom offered him a job at his farm implement business, and Phyllis opened a bedroom for him while he was on probation. Another young man came from a broken home and had no financial support for his dream of college. Again, they extended an offer of a job and housing. Along with housing came that one-on-one exposure to how they lived out their faith in Jesus. "A few months ago we learned that this second boy and his family have come to faith in Christ," Phyllis said. "What he saw and heard have come to life. It's so exciting. It makes it worthwhile."

They rejoice, too, over the happy ending for a young woman in their town who was checking groceries when they met. Phyllis had overheard her tell another customer that she needed housing. She'd left home at fifteen when her parents divorced and didn't have much of a future. "Would you like to live with us?" Phyllis asked the stunned girl as she went through the checkout line. The girl asked to come out for an interview.

"We live in a small town and I'm sure she knew that we were considered 'religious' people," Phyllis said. "When she came out, she told us she didn't smoke or drink and would like to live with us. That was June. In November she accepted Christ into her life." Her bond to Phyllis and Tom grew so strong that she's become like a daughter to them, and they're helping her through college. "We'll have her for the rest of our lives," Phyllis said.

Another unexpected hospitality time came through Phyllis's ministry of writing letters of spiritual counsel to troubled people whose stories she read in the newspaper. One was "Nita," daughter of alcoholics and hardened street child, who at nineteen already had been in fourteen foster homes and had a four-inch-thick file of prostitution and drug offenses. When Nita was released pending admission to an addiction treatment facility, she had no place to go. She knew only one person who cared—Phyllis, who'd written her for two months. One afternoon the sheriff's office called Phyllis; by dusk a deputy dropped off Nita with only the clothes on her back, a list of law-enforcement numbers, and strict orders to keep her under twenty-four-hour surveillance for the next few days. Her stay extended more than a month.

"We put her in a bedroom in the basement," Phyllis recalled. "When we heard the door to the outside open, we didn't know if it was just her going outside to smoke or her attempting to run away. But she was very considerate and fit right in. We sat down to dinner together—something she'd missed in all her years of street living. We took her to church and to work. She even got up with me at 4 A.M. for my rodeo trips.

"She also revealed to us her deep involvement in major drug crime," Phyllis added. "We didn't sleep very well that month, knowing we had a hardened criminal under our roof. But she was always respectful."

Nita accepted Christ and began to grow spiritually while with them, but eventually returned to the streets and further jail time. She never forgot them, however. A jail chaplain's assistant told them how Nita always talked about her time with them. Then one day at a local restaurant they ran into her again. She was attending church and getting help for her addictions. "Our encounter had to be of the Lord," Phyllis said.

Meanwhile, more lives are being touched through Phyllis and Tom's hospitality. Their good reputation in the rodeo culture and their gracious concern for people open doors in unexpected ways. One summer they took in two thirteen-year-old girls. The parents of one girl were divorcing; the other simply enjoyed being around Phyllis. They practiced racing their horses around barrels in the corral, but in between came time for life-changing talks—all because a caring woman extended hospitality.

The Lord's Blessing

Every Gospel writer records that sacred moment when Jesus looked up to heaven and gave thanks before breaking the loaves and fishes for distribution. What a special moment that was, as God the Son acknowledged provision from God the Father. I chastise my kids when they rush through the table prayer like pigs racing to a feed trough or if they groan about whose "turn" it is to "have to pray."

It's a privilege to pause before the God of all provision, acknowledging that this meal is both fuel for the body and renewal for the soul. My family holds hands while praying before a meal, even when non-Christian guests are present. I think it symbolizes our unity in seeking the Lord's blessing on our relationships.

The Lord *does* bless us when others join us for a meal. I'm not the world's fanciest cook and our ten-by-sixteen combination kitchen–dining room is rather cramped. We often practice the "extra plate" hospitality, which means quickly dumping an extra potato in the pot or eating a little less so the food stretches. One time we had two extra, unplanned guests: a single friend and an older widow. The menu was truly humble: cabbage and sausage! But afterward, my single friend remarked, "I'm so glad you invited me. My meals are so quiet!" My young children, who had the manners of puppies, certainly kept the meal "unquiet." The widow remarked, "It means so much to an old lady like me to be included."

Other times, my meals have a little more finesse, with a white tablecloth and my late mother's china. We "pull out the stops," for example, when we celebrate the birthdays of a child and his single mother who otherwise wouldn't have a party. "I can't believe you'd roast a turkey just for me," she said one year as I rushed around stirring gravy and mashing potatoes at the last minute. Yes, I would—because I want this mother and her son to know they are special to the Lord.

I believe the Lord especially wants to bless the hospitality that targets the widow, the orphan, and the alien, who in Old Testament times were singled out for special protection. In our mobile, broken society, that includes single parents and their children plus others who have no family support system nearby. I read of a woman who was at a spiritual and emotional low after her husband left her with teenagers to raise. One night friends planned a "just because" party in her honor, with gifts and decorations picking up the theme of teddy bears, a favorite of hers. She was touched and encouraged.

Don't Expect a Thank-you Note

My mother taught me to follow up every expression of hospitality with a thank-you note. I'm not perfect, but I think I do better than the people whom Jesus fed by the Sea of Galilee. Afterward, instead of expressing gratitude, these people tried to force him to be their king. They weren't interested in spiritual food. They just wanted a permanent welfare system with Miracle Bread.

We still run into those attitudes. A couple I'll call Lee and Margaret did when they reached out to a drifter, "Manny," who stopped in their town in pain that required a dentist's help. The Christian dentist and his receptionist sensed Manny wanted to change his life. The receptionist called her husband, who spent some time with Manny, explaining the gospel. Then he called his pastor, Lee, to see what practical help the church could offer. Together, they again talked with Manny about becoming a Christian.

"Our church could only buy him food," Lee recalled. "It didn't have housing for him. So we offered him our own guest bedroom. I wouldn't do the same today. I'd be more afraid of my wife and children's safety. But then it seemed right. He genuinely seemed to want to conquer his alcoholism and start over."

Lee rented a chainsaw and hired Manny to prepare a pile of firewood. The receptionist's husband had Manny help him stripe a parking lot. But nobody else seemed to want to hire a hobo, especially in late fall when harvest was over. As weeks passed, Lee and Margaret simply included Manny in their Christian family life.

"He was kind and respectful to my wife and children," Lee said. "We gave him unconditional love. We trusted him and he rose to our trust." Lee and Margaret even let Manny use their car—to the surprise of a transient friend he brought for Thanksgiving dinner. His friend wasn't as trustworthy; he rummaged through the medicine cabinet in their bathroom looking for drugs.

Then one day, on the verge of taking a part-time janitorial job, Manny packed up and said good-bye. He re-entered their lives a few times after that—once, calling for bus fare to get to a drug treatment center, two other times for food. In the last meeting, Manny walked away in anger after Lee turned down a request for extra money, suspecting he'd probably use it for drink.

"He knows about the Lord," Lee says. "He saw it in our lives." Manny left behind one memory of his sojourn, a coffee mug that he took to Alcoholics Anonymous meetings. Lee keeps it in his office as a reminder of Jesus' call to minister "to the least of these." The Lord established that criteria one Sabbath day when his dinner at the house of a Pharisee turned into a sham. Right off, some Pharisees clicked their tongues when Jesus healed a man of dropsy— on the Sabbath, no less! Then Jesus noticed how guests fought over the places of honor. Exasperated, Jesus criticized them for limiting their guest lists to relatives, friends, and rich neighbors. Instead, he said, they should invite "the poor, the crippled, the lame, the blind, and you will be blessed. Although they cannot repay you, you will be repaid at the resurrection of the righteous" (Luke 14:13-14).

One Thanksgiving, when I was still single, some friends did exactly that. They cooked up a nice turkey meal and included among the guests a polio survivor, another who was "lame" in mind, and another who was blind. Then they included me and two seminary friends—I guess we qualified as "poor"! But I think we need to broaden Jesus' terms to include those who are emotionally poor, crippled, or blind.

When I was living in a cramped one-bedroom apartment, I got a call one night from somebody who'd written to my newspaper recipe column. She was down at the bus depot with her two small children. Her marriage had fallen apart, and she was headed to her parents' home. The bus depot was closing for the night, and she had no money for a motel. My apartment was so tiny I could open the refrigerator and oven while sitting at the table. (During the years that I was "Food Editor" of the small-town daily, people couldn't believe that I didn't have a fancy "test kitchen"!) But God moved me to bring this family home. I fed them, opened my third-hand sofa-bed, and found enough bedding for all of them. I helped rock the frightened children to sleep, then prayed with the mother. On my way to work the next morning, I took them back to the bus depot. I never heard from her again and perhaps will never know until eternity the rest of her story.

A few years later, as a short-term missionary, I again had a tiny one-bedroom apartment. Twice, young women with medical or emotional problems needed a place to stay. That meant one of us slept on the plastic sofa—quite a rude awakening when you turned over and slipped to the floor! Their problems definitely stretched me, but I knew I'd obeyed the Lord's instruction to share what I had.

God is honored when we reach out to special groups of hurting people. They may not practice the etiquette of sending thank-yous, but our reward will come from heaven.

Singles
Ever eat tuna casserole for five days straight? This is one fact of my single lifestyle I hate to confess. How I loved a home-cooked meal and banter with a real family. One time I talked a mom into including me for dinner instead of paying me cash for her son's weekly violin lesson. Johnny didn't practice much, but his mother was a great cook! And have you ever thought how Sunday afternoons are some of the loneliest times of the week for singles?

The Grieving
The traumas of death, illness, or marital struggle can

greatly affect a person's health. Right after my parents died, I didn't feel like cooking or eating, and my weight plummeted. I was the living illustration of Psalm 102:3-7, which among other things describes a "pelican of the wilderness" (NASB). A pelican that hasn't had its tank full of fish is a pretty desperate-looking creature! But getting invited to somebody's home for a meal gave me a much-needed break from probate and clean out. It was especially nice when they sent leftovers home with me. I fussed outwardly, but I savored every bite of those love dishes.

The Alienated

One February morning at college we received the shocking news that the boyfriend of the girl who lived upstairs had killed himself. This happened just a few days before the campus sweetheart banquet. Some of us without dates decided to spare this girl the trauma of being excluded from this event, which she had expected to attend. We snatched her away from campus early and took her to a nice restaurant, then to a sacred concert. It didn't take away her hurt, of course, but our expression of love helped pour a little of the Lord's balm into her wounded heart.

The Lord's Choice

God used a widow's unpretentious hospitality to firm up my faith. Soon after I started my first newspaper job, a retired nurse named Halcyon sought me out after church and in her no-nonsense way invited me home for dinner at her little brown cottage. She loved Jesus, and she loved to share what she'd read in her Bible, so worn out that it molded itself to her knees. Our Sunday-dinner friendship eventually became Friday night "laundry and leftovers." My apartment had no washing facilities, and the downtown Laundromat was not safe for a young woman at night. So I'd bring over my spaghetti leftovers, she'd add in her homemade yogurt and whole wheat bread, and we'd feast while I did my wash. I left my washer quarters in a piggy bank to compensate for water and electricity costs. But they were meager payment for the greater investment she made in me as we became friends.

We get so hung up on "where we live" and "what we eat." Jesus knew about these human weaknesses. At the beginning of his ministry, he was walking along when two men came up and said, "Rabbi, . . . where are you staying?" (John 1:38). Perhaps they added, "Hey, does it have a pool? how about a barbecue? or at least a stereo with a bunch of CDs? Let's crank up the volume! Yeah, a Christian group so everybody gets the message!" Of course not! Jesus probably had some tiny dirt-floored room with just the basics. The key was that he simply invited them to his temporary abode. After they saw what little there was to "see," they spent the day with him. Not admiring his decor or raving over his cooking. Just being with the Lord of Lords. That's hospitality—God style.

Groomed to Bloom

1. Imagine getting through a chapter on hospitality without mentioning Mary and Martha! Well, here they are. Reread the account of Martha's showdown in Luke 10:38-42. Decide how Martha was dissatisfied, demanding, distrustful, and distracted. What do you think Jesus meant by "only one thing is needed"?

2. The principle for showing "brotherly love toward strangers" (the literal meaning of *philoxenia*) originates in a command in Leviticus 19:34. What was the context of that command and how might it still be true of today's circumstances? Read Isaiah 58:7 for clues.

3. Hebrews 13:2 tells us to show hospitality to strangers, "for by so doing some people have entertained angels without knowing it." Can you give a biblical example of this happening? How might it happen today? Consider Matthew 25:37-40 in your answer.

4. What principles for hospitality are expressed in 1 Peter

4:9, especially when read with 1 Samuel 25:2-38? Check out the résumés for potential church leaders in 1 Timothy 3:2 and Titus 1:8 and a spiritual checkpoint offered for godly widows in 1 Timothy 5:10.

5. Hospitality is considered a debt of love. Memorize this verse: "Share with God's people who are in need. Practice hospitality" (Rom. 12:13).

8

Lotza Zuc to Share

The Encouragement of Giving

There's nothing like a healthy zucchini plant to make everybody a close friend. Zucchini do not practice birth control. You plant these innocent little seeds and before you can turn around twice and do an Irish jig, vines are crawling all over your garden. Shades of monster movies, where the slime crushes doors and pushes out walls! Underneath the vines, little legless iguanas begin forming. Before you know it, you have enough to feed a football team plus a few extras for scrimmage.

That's when you bless the church's "Share Your Garden" table. Your car groans to the front door of the church where you gleefully unload these obese green things that could pass for watermelons. Surely, some joyful soul will take home all thirty of them and gratefully dine for a month on zucchini casserole.

I grew up on zucchini casserole. And zuc muffins, zuc bread, zuc salad . . . more than anything else, except maybe a bumper crop of prunes, zucchini brings out the giver in us. We don't mind sharing what we have in abundance. But it's a different matter when God asks us to give something more costly or hard to replace. A little detail about a donkey, included in three of the Gospels, provides some counsel for the encouragement of giving.

It was time for Jesus to start to wind up his ministry and enter Jerusalem as its Messiah. He didn't have an army or an impressive entourage to precede him into the capital city. All he had were some worn-out sandals. But finding a steed was no problem for the Son of God. He told his disciples to toddle on up to the next village, where they'd find a donkey and her colt, which nobody had ever ridden before. They were to untie the colt and bring it to him. If anybody asked, they were to say, "The Lord needs it."

The Lord needs it. That's the bottom line for the ministry of giving. We yield things of value to God so that he can place them where they are needed. Four principles guide the ministry of giving:

- If you need something, God knows—but tell him anyway.
- If you have it, God gave it to you.
- If God needs to reassign it, obey him.
- If it's a secret, keep the secret.

Tell Him Your Need

Children are good at telling you their needs. Especially at Christmas! We had our years of "Dear Santa" letters on the refrigerator, even though as children raised on the manger story, they knew better. Then there were birthdays, those once-a-year King- or Queen-for-a-Day occasions when they got breakfast in bed and the dinner menu of their choice. Jesus knew he'd be hailed King for the Day as he neared Jerusalem for the last week of his life. He knew how quickly the people's accolades would turn into accusations bringing on his betrayal, condemnation, and crucifixion. But for this moment he needed appropriate transportation. He didn't want a horse, the symbol of a conquering king. He wanted the humble donkey that fulfilled the prophecy in Zechariah 9:9 of a King of Peace. He didn't have to check the phone book or the want ads to fulfill this need. With his perfect knowledge and complete authority, he just knew it would be ready for him.

God operates the same way with us. Our needs come as no surprise to him. He sees the past, the present, and the future. But he still wants us to tell him about our needs, so he can teach us to trust him. My friend Mary discovered that many times in her life, but she'll always remember one particular incident in rural Kentucky in the 1950s. Her family was living on a farm that couldn't support them. One night she put her children to bed with an extra heavy heart, knowing that they had no food for breakfast.

"I was truly at the end of myself," she says. "We had no phone, and our neighbors were miles away, separated by gullies and ridges. A store was just as far away. But it wouldn't have done much good. I didn't have money to buy food."

Mary stoked the fire in their kitchen, then shut herself in a frigid spare room. Kneeling by its only furniture, an old bedstead, she spent a long time in prayer before going to bed. When morning came, she paced the floor, trying to keep warm and knowing she'd soon have to go outside and search for branches and lumber scraps for the kitchen fire. Even without food, they needed heat. Glancing outside, she was surprised to see somebody coming up the lane so early on such a cold morning. She was shocked to see it was Kathreen, a mother of two who lived a three-mile walk away on the next ridge. Many times Mary had taken that walk to visit Kathreen, who was virtually bedridden with tuberculosis.

"I couldn't believe she'd come in her condition," Mary said, "nor could I believe what she'd brought. She put two jars of green beans, a slab of bacon, and three ears of popcorn on my table. I'd prayed for food, but I never expected it to come by Kathreen, least of all on a bone-chilling morning."

Mary will never forget that breakfast of popcorn floating on green beans and bacon. Eventually, Mary's circum-stances improved. A relative began sending money for gro-ceries. Later, they moved away, and a few years after that she learned Kathreen had died of TB. But she'll never forget how God used a sick woman to confirm that he knew Mary's desperate need.

Stories like Mary's remind me that God truly cares about my needs. I may have my "want" list—and advertisers do a good job of trying to tell me that my wants are really needs. I'm a veteran of declining phone offers for siding and credit cards. And I have to resist flipping through mail-order catalogs with brightly colored pictures that shout "Buy me! Buy me!" In the Lord's Prayer we ask, "Give us this day our daily bread"—not our daily chocolate eclairs. When God allows a lean time in our lives, it's to cut away the fat of too many wants. "Better the little that the right-eous have than the wealth of many wicked" warns Psalm 37:16. When we come to the point of seeing the difference between needs and wants, God has our hearts ready to receive his blessing.

What You Have Is God's

As a child, I loved hearing how Jesus knew just where to find the donkey he needed. But the next part of the story always bothered me. I'd been duly indoctrinated against stealing, such that I was afraid to go near the cookie jar or even sniff those tempting flowers in the neighbor's yard. I wouldn't even think of jumping on the neighbor kid's bike without permission. How could God, who commanded us not to steal, have his Son "steal" a donkey? The answer comes from the people's reaction as the disciples untied the animal from the doorway. At first they objected, "What are you doing, untying that colt?" When the disciples said, "The Lord has need of it," they let them go. Jesus' reputa-tion was enough assurance. Perhaps they'd already been blessed in some way by his ministry. They knew this great Teacher would treat the animal kindly and return it.

More importantly, he could not steal what was already his. Psalm 50:10 says God owns the cattle on a thousand hills. Cowboys may burn their brands into the hides of those critters, but God is the ultimate owner of all that we have. That donkey really belonged to the Lord, and the villagers who fed and used it were just its earthly caregivers. The same principle goes for any of our so-called possessions. God is asking, "What's in your stall?"

Often, God is looking at our wallets. First Timothy 6:18 advises the rich to be generous and ready to share. A contemporary example of that was R. G. LeTourneau, the engineering and machinery genius who made millions, established a Christian college, and reportedly gave 90 percent of his income to the Lord's work. Yet we can all apply a principle he shared: "The question is not how much of my money I give to God," he said, "but rather how much of God's money I keep for myself."[1] A similar attitude was expressed by Maxey Jarman, who built a billion-dollar corporation, Genesco. When reverses came, he continued to contribute generously to Christian ministries. One time a close friend asked him if he ever thought of the millions he gave away. "Of course I have," Jarman replied, "but remember, I didn't lose a penny I gave away. I only lost what I kept."[2]

But Romans 12:13 includes the other end of the economic spectrum with its simple command: "Share with God's people who are in need." I experienced the spiritual richness of this command when I was raising support for mission service. One of the first to pledge was a man who was poor by the world's standards—on support himself with a home mission project. When I objected, saying he needed it more, he replied, "God keeps shoveling it in and I keep shoveling it out." Later, during my mission service, a couple in a rural area sent a check with this note: "The Lord gave us a good weekend at a little fruit stand we put up by the road. Here's the Lord's part, and we want it for you." Another family often sent a one-time gift in the spring, about the time when income tax returns got processed. The check was usually an odd-dollar amount, and I often wondered if they had simply turned over a tithe of their tax refund. Such gifts reminded me again that these people regarded the Lord as the origin of their income and gave accordingly.

God's giving isn't limited to money. He can use just about anything. One friend saw God divert part of a cherry crop. She'd moved to our town just as cherries ripened and was thrilled with the prospect of canning some for winter. But she got so busy settling in and mothering her three kids that she didn't have time to can. Then one morning, she went to the front door and found eighteen quarts of canned cherries lined up outside. They came from a woman whose energies were already taxed with care for her invalid husband. My friend's family savored every quart that winter, knowing how much sacrifice went into the gift.

Another time the same friend and her husband needed a getaway as a couple yet couldn't afford much. Another family lent them their large motor home, even stocking the refrigerator with snacks. The crowning touch was a rose and love note secured to the counter of the kitchen area.

Most of us have closets and rooms crowded with excess clothes, home furnishings, or just plain "stuff." When word got out that I welcomed scraps to sew my kids' clothes, I was inundated by boxes of fabric. For years my children wore made-for-almost-nothing "originals" until puberty's self-consciousness set in. I still wear a dress I sewed for twenty-five cents (the cost of a zipper at the thrift store) from fabric given me. My family was also blessed when bags of used clothes came our way. A growth spurt later, those bagfuls of gently worn clothes made a trip to homes of other children. One summer my husband came home from cherry harvest with news that some migrant workers he supervised had their tent burglarized and all their clothes stolen. He pulled shirts and pants out of his closet, loaded a box, and took them to the men. Even after sharing, our closet was still full enough.

At one retreat where I spoke on giving, I was ap-

proached by a woman who confessed to being overwhelmed by "stuff." Her house and garage were piled high,
and she had more in a storage unit. She warmed to my
idea that she ask a friend help her sort (the buddy system is
a great way to pare down) and pass along what she didn't
need to people who had little or nothing, like the immigrants arriving in great numbers in her community.

I recall hearing that John Wesley went through his belongings yearly. If he hadn't used something in a year, he
passed it on. "He who gives to the poor," says Proverbs
28:27, "will lack nothing, but he who closes his eyes to
them receives many curses." That's a good reminder for
letting God clean out the contents of our lives.

Let God Reassign It

We often miss a little detail about the "triumphal entry"
colt. It hadn't been ridden before! Yet the disciples threw
their cloaks on it as a makeshift saddle and Jesus climbed
on. Anybody else might have been bucked off. But this
critter didn't balk at all over carrying its Creator into Jerusalem. When God assigns your money or goods to somebody else, he will take care of the details. The timing and
amount will be just right.

I heard such a story from Dagmar, a petite German lady
who has supported herself with jobs as a maid or caregiver.
For four years, until it proved too much physically, she was
a housekeeper at a Christian camp. Then one summer day,
long after she'd quit working at the camp, she received a
cashier's check for $500 from a church that supported the
camp. "I'd never gone to services at that church," she said,
"so I couldn't understand why I received that gift." When
she asked at the camp office about the gift, one of the
workers just shrugged her shoulders and said, "Don't worry
about it. Someone or a group of people felt a prompting by
the Holy Spirit and acted accordingly." Dagmar put the
check in her savings account, wrote a thank-you note "to

whom it may concern," and asked God to bless the givers—whoever they were.

Two weeks later she developed dental problems. She had no insurance to cover the $540 bill—but she did have that gift in her savings. "I praised the Lord and thanked him for being so good to me," she said. "I felt so unworthy of this gift. But God showed me through this how much he loved me. God is so awesome! Sometimes he provides right on time and sometimes just ahead!"

Dagmar feels especially drawn to Paul's prayer in Ephesians 3:14-21, which talks about the glorious riches of knowing God's power and love. It's often through such incidents of human giving that we begin to grasp the width, length, height, and depth of God's love for us. Our giving is so puny compared with his greatest gift to mankind—salvation through the death of his Son. When gifts come our way, our response should be that of Paul: "Thanks be to God for his indescribable gift!" (2 Cor. 9:15).

When we view giving as part of our response to God's love, it's easier to let him reassign what we have to others. We've tried to impress that principle on our children by becoming sponsors in compassion ministries. Our children were young when we began sponsoring a girl in Haiti. I put her picture on our missionary bulletin board, and when my kids showed playmates around the house, they often pointed out the picture of "my extra sister in Haiti." It was quite a testimony for kids who didn't come from Christian homes!

During our ten years of sponsorship, our children prayed for her nearly every night. When she left school, we took on another Haitian child, plus a boy in central Africa whose pastor-father was killed in the ethnic massacres. Our kids know that Dad writes a check every month to help these children go to school and have one meal a day. Their stiff, posed photos in well-worn clothes remind us of their poverty. So do their translated letters, which often tell us how they used extra money gifts for food for their families. I realized this project was helping teach my children the importance of sharing when my son, then twelve, came to me with extra money he'd earned substituting on a paper route. "Please send this to our kids next month," he told me. His action reminded me of how Paul commended the poor Christians of the Macedonian church for giving "even beyond their ability" to help other poor Christians in Jerusalem (2 Cor. 8:3). More important than "how much" we have is the proportion we share.

Sometimes, rather than giving something away, God simply asks us to share it. Summers in our town get rather hot, but we are exceedingly blessed by friends who leave us in charge of their lovely home when they go away. The cat needs to be fed, the roses must be watered—and their beautiful in-ground pool needs chlorine added and the water "stirred up." We do a good job of that! Other families also get pool invites, a prized earthly pleasure for those of us whose "pools" otherwise would be the type that fold up into a box and cost twenty dollars.

At times in my life I've been encouraged by the loan of a mattress to sleep on when I didn't even have a bed, a car to move to an apartment when I was without wheels, and even the veil I wore for my economy wedding. When I returned these items with a grateful heart, the owners often said, "No problem. I know you'd do the same for somebody else."

The late Henrietta Mears took that attitude when she dug into her own purse to help the young seminary students who packed her large Sunday school class at Hollywood's First Presbyterian Church. She had a deserved reputation as an excellent Bible teacher. But she also had a big heart for these young men and bought many their first "preacher's suits" and winter overcoats. She told them to think of the gifts simply as loans and that someday they could do the same for others.[3]

Keep the Secret

Our culture is great for naming animals. You take a walk

and meet somebody holding a leash attached to a glob of fur the size of an artichoke. If you ask, "What's your dog's name?" get ready for something like this: "Mortimer Ulysses Tyrone Theobald" (whom they call "Mutt" for short). When neighbors go on vacation, we feed their fussy, feeble, twenty-year-old feline named "Ninety-Nine," who's been through that many lives. After hearing his father explain what he was cleaning out of a fresh catch of fish, my son, then five, named one of his first goldfish "Gut." One classroom pet we took home over long school weekends was a gerbil aptly named "Houdini." It didn't survive to the end of school. One weekend at another classmate's home, it escaped the cage, never to be seen again. Was that a big smile on the family dog's face?

No name, however, is given to one of the most famous animals in the Bible. The donkey that Jesus rode into Jerusalem is just a donkey. We don't even know his owner's name. But neither name matters. The role of "givers" is not to bring attention to themselves but to connect the recipients with God. A. W. Tozer illustrated this by telling the Palm Sunday story with the focus on the donkey. As the critter heard the loud hosannas and saw coats and palm branches spread before him, he flicked a fly off a mange patch and said, "I had no idea they really appreciated me like this! Listen to those hosannas, would you. I must really be something."[4] Of course that didn't happen! But if we, as donkeys or loaners of donkeys, think the praise should come to us, we've got the ministry of giving all wrong.

Annie had her priorities right when she and another woman teamed up to clean the house of a friend whose life was out of control with marital problems and hospitalizations. As she changed sheets, Annie noticed the bed's shabby spread. She also thought of how that bedspread might bring bad memories of a sour marriage. She'd just been given a large amount of fabric and had ten dollars extra for "mad money." She bought batting with the money and sewed for two solid days to make the woman a new bedspread. There was no way she could sneak it in the house. So she quietly delivered it to her friend, who hugged her and asked, "How can I ever thank you?" Annie replied, "Just thank the Lord."

Other times it's better not to know the origin of a love gift, so that praise for the gift absolutely goes to the Lord. That's why Jesus warned against behaving like the Pharisees, who crowed from the street corners about all their almsgiving. They had their reward in tooting their own horns. They had their egos stroked. But people who give in secret bring special delight to God.

Patty and Kent have a story to tell about that. One fall they needed an extra car, so they invested $1,300 in one with high miles and a record of good care. It was a lot of money for them, and they felt good about their purchase. At Christmas they drove the car to his parents' home, but during that three-hour trip they started hearing ominous sounds in the car's transmission. It drank transmission fluid like a thirsty nomad. By the time they got to their destination, they knew they had major problems. A mechanic confirmed their fears: the car needed a transmission job costing $1,300—what they'd paid for the car in the first place.

"We were so discouraged," said Patty. "This was right at Christmas and we didn't have money like that. Kent's dad loaned us the money to fix it, but we still needed to pay it back. Kent and I felt led to ask some people to pray that God would show us how to earn this money."

A few weeks later Patty was greeted at the mailbox by a neighbor. "I have something to give you," she said, emphasizing it came from someone who wanted to remain anonymous. Patty was in a hurry and didn't open the envelope for a few hours. When she did, her knees nearly buckled under her. Someone had typed out 1 John 3:17-18: "If anyone has material possessions and sees his brother in need but has no pity on him, how can the love of God be in him? Dear children, let us not love with words or tongue but with actions and in truth." The note was signed: "We beheld your need. Love from the family of God." The senders had enclosed a check for more than $1,600. Ten days later, also anonymously, there came another check for $300. The amount remaining after paying back the transmission bill enabled Kent and Patty to make needed repairs on their other vehicle.

"My first reaction was to find out who gave us that money," Patty said. "Then we realized that we simply needed to accept it as from God. It was humbling to be loved so much and to see how God could take care of us."

Gifts like the money sent to Patty and Kent tend to multiply in other ways. They're involved in youth ministry, and their story of how God supplied is getting planted in lots of young and receptive hearts. Like zucchini vines, you never know how far or how much that gift will reproduce!

Groomed to Bloom

1. The biggest snare to a ministry of giving is pride. Read about the heart of the first church in Acts 4:32-37 (including the gift of the "Son of Encouragement"), then move on to the story of Ananias and Sapphira in Acts 5:1-10. What principle can you pull from their tragic story?

2. In the Old Testament, wealth was often associated with God's blessing. Yet some of the most "blessed" people are those who have little materially. What trait of righteousness is revealed in Psalm 37:25-26?

3. Have you ever been around someone who's poor yet very generous? Read 2 Corinthians 8:1-15, where Paul upholds the poor Macedonians as an example of generous giving. What phrase in that passage especially touches you as a challenge to give? How does this relate to James 2:14-17?

4. Put into your own words the equation for giving in

Luke 6:38. Share a time when that has happened in your life.

5. Ponder this promise for givers: "A generous man will himself be blessed, for he shares his food with the poor" (Prov. 22:9).

9

Have Trowel, Will Travel

The Encouragement of Helping

We need to update the old-fashioned custom of barn raising with one tailored to those of us afflicted with weeds. We've all read about days when a whole slate of friends and relatives show up for fun disguised as work. While the womenfolk fry up chicken and stir up raisin pie, the menfolk muscle up four walls and a roof in time for dinner. Why not host similar parties to transform our yards from ratty to resplendent? I'll gladly supply trowels, trimmers, trash bags, and treats!

Until then, you'll find me at Grandma's, mowing her lawn while 35,000 dandelions commit an act of yellow sabotage in mine. I shouldn't complain. Years ago, when Grandpa was still alive, the roles were reversed. At the time we were a two-crib household. I'd look outside as I folded diapers and bemoan my scraggly yard. Then Grandpa arrived with his long-handled poker to dislodge every last dandelion in the lawn. Grandma grabbed her trowel, got down on her knees in my briar patch, and restored it to a rose garden.

When life throws us more weeds than we can handle—whether they're financial, physical, or emotional—we feel a tremendous boost when somebody comes to our side with practical service. Such was the case of two Old Testament widows, Naomi and Ruth. Their story shows both the high personal cost and the reward of this way to encourage people. Helping asks that we

- walk alongside somebody who hurts,
- see ourselves as part of the solution,
- stoop to serve with ordinary skills, and
- let God work out the synergy.

Walking alongside the Hurting

Most people think of the Old Testament book of Ruth as a touching love story that also holds deep, prophetic symbolism of Christ our Redeemer. It struck me another way the winter I was thirty-three. An old boyfriend had been in touch after eight years of silence, and his letters and calls were getting rather serious. In my Bible read-through, I came to Ruth 3:18: "For the man will not rest until the matter is settled today." My old boyfriend settled it and changed my residence and name! The event left many people breathless, but nowhere near what Ruth went through when she left her native land with her widowed mother-in-law, Naomi.

Their story began years earlier, during a famine in which Naomi, her husband, and two sons left Judah for greener pastures in a pagan land, Moab. The sons subsequently married women from Moab, Ruth and Orpah. Then the father and both sons died, leaving three widows. When Naomi decided to return to Judah, her daughters-in-law started out with her. But one proved a "leaver" and the other a "cleaver." Orpah turned back, understandably apprehensive about going to an unknown land where she would be ostracized because of her nationality. But Ruth hung in there with Naomi: "Where you go I will go . . . your people will be my people."

We tend to frame that verse with wedding satin and roses. But it really wasn't that romantic in context. Naomi was no bluebird of cheer. It wasn't "Happy Trails" she crooned as she and Ruth started trudging back to Bethlehem. It was "Mournful Wails." Along the way she decided to change her name to Mara, meaning "bitter." Her life had turned bitter, and nothing good awaited her in her homeland except dying among her own people.

But there's a quiet key to Ruth's character in a verse we often race over: "So the two women went on until they came to Bethlehem" (Ruth 1:19). We're not told Naomi's age, but she was at least old enough to be done with childbearing and certainly not Boston Marathon material. Neither are we told how they traveled, whether by foot or by donkey. As the crow flies, Moab was more than fifty miles southeast of Bethlehem, but the road hooked around the top of the Dead Sea before dropping into Moabite territory. It was a long, hot, arduous journey for two women alone, carrying their essential life possessions. But they "went on," day after day.

Sometimes God calls us to the difficult "day after day" role in another's life. We're to be the Ruths alongside people whose lives are so torn by tragedy that we simply don't know how to ease their pain. Ruth was a risk taker of tremendous depth when she went on that long hike to an unknown land with a downcast old woman. Her motivation is revealed in her reply, "Your God will be my God." During her marriage, Ruth had learned enough about Naomi's God to choose to turn away from her idolatrous heritage. Even Naomi's bitter grieving couldn't shake Ruth's adoptive faith. She believed that, somehow, God would supply their needs. Encouragers are like that. When they get around people whose own faith umbrellas are tattered, they open another, bigger umbrella over both of them. Such is the admonition of Philippians 2:4: "Each of you should look not only to your own interests, but also to the interests of others."

"Walking alongside" isn't always in our script. With a toddler and baby at home, Annie lived from diaper change to diaper change and collapsed in bed at night. Then she learned of an unmarried career woman in her church who was pregnant and abandoned by her boyfriend. "My first thought was somebody ought to help her," Annie said. "I didn't know her very well, but God seemed to tell me I was the one to do it." Her resulting commitment to be the woman's "birth coach" then embraced invitations to meals on the night of childbirth classes and even mowing the small lawn around the woman's mobile home, just before and after delivery. "I pulled into her car port, opened the car doors so I could watch my babies in their car seats, and mowed like crazy for twenty minutes," Annie remembers.

Diana found herself literally walking alongside a needy friend in the aftermath of a freak windstorm that blew apart the friend's hillside mobile home, scattering possessions throughout nearby orchards. They walked together in the mud, gathering things, and then Diana took her to the laundromat to wash what could be saved. She also did her part as concerned people helped the friend and her disabled husband refurbish another temporary place to live.

Another Diana, a pastor's wife with a baby and a toddler, was dragging physically and emotionally through her third pregnancy. Then Marie, a college student, told her she had declared her next day off as "Diana Day" and she would help in any way for free. The student invested her day cleaning an oven, vacuuming, and ironing, and giving Diana a boost.

Ruth—an older, appropriately named friend—encouraged me when she walked me through the process of disposing of my parents' belongings. I was numb when they died, leaving a three-bedroom home full of the accumulations of people raised in the save-everything Depression era. Before each of the seven garage sales, Ruth came over to coach me on pricing things and comfort me when I cried. Then she came for the first hour or two of each sale to help when the crowds were the thickest. It wasn't easy for her, either, since she was a close friend of my parents. And even though, like Naomi, I was tempted to call myself

Mara, the embittered one, she willingly involved herself in this hard part of my life.

Becoming Part of the Solution

Sometimes, when I get a little behind in housework, my son or daughter comes to me with a frantic countenance and desperate plea: "Mom, my very favorite shirt is in the hamper and I want to wear it tomorrow!" Though I haven't quite finished training them in the 'fine art of pushing buttons on the washing machine, I'm trying hard to teach them to approach problems believing they can be part of the solution.

I don't want them to grow up like some seminary students who flunked an embarrassing *Candid Camera*–type test. Some researchers selected forty ministerial students under the pretense of doing a survey on careers in the church. They asked each student to walk to a nearby building where they would dictate into a tape recorder an impromptu talk on either the Good Samaritan story or their concern for a career. On the way, researchers planted an actor who would groan and collapse as the seminarian approached. More than half of the students walked right on by! "Some, who were planning their dissertation on the Good Samaritan," the report said, "literally stepped over the slumped body as they hurried along."[1]

Thankfully, when Ruth and Naomi arrived in Bethlehem, Ruth didn't ignore their urgent survival needs. Because Naomi's late husband had apparently mortgaged the family property, they were reduced to handouts. But they had arrived at the beginning of barley harvest, and Levitical law allowed the poor to glean. Ruth took the initiative: "Let me go to the fields and pick up the leftover grain behind anyone in whose eyes I find favor" (Ruth 2:2). She showed great courage in venturing out where everything was so new and confusing. Whenever I moved somewhere, I lived for months by a map. I feared getting lost between home and the grocery store! But Ruth had more than geography to deal with. Her new home had a different language and culture. She would be quickly recognized as a foreigner and perhaps shunned. But she did not let these negatives discourage her.

The real test of a helper-encourager is willingness to get involved. It's easy to let somebody else do it—and usually that somebody else is experiencing "helping overload." God intended that we share in helping those in need: "Therefore, as we have opportunity, let us do good to all people, especially to those who belong to the family of believers" (Gal. 6:10). We're often willing to pray about a need. But sometimes God wants us to get off our knees and off to the need!

My neighbor Terri models that for me. She's one of those organized women who cooks casseroles ahead for her family and for ministry. Consider the October Monday that life crushed in on me. The previous night we had come home in a rented car after an out-of-state minivacation ended in a serious auto accident. We came close to being killed when the other driver sped across the center line of a mountain highway, totaling our car. As I started phoning doctors for appointments, Terri came to the door with a casserole and a willingness to help in whatever way needed. Two more meals came from Georgia, another friend from church whose heart hurt over our "Mara" experience. I welcomed her food and savored her hugs of consolation. I was also grateful for the thoughtfulness of both women in delivering those meals in disposable containers. I had so much going on, I was glad I didn't have to return dishes.

We can't meet every need out there, but God will usually put a real heaviness in our hearts when there's something we ought to do. Scott found that true as he came to the end of himself one hot, weary summer night. For months he had pursued the dream of building his family an adequate home after years in cramped rentals. During the days, he expended his energies as a builder on other people's homes. Evenings and weekends, he went to his own lot and nailed and sawed until it was so dark he couldn't see any more. Many times friends came to help. But he will never forget the night he was all alone, installing sidewalk forms for cement pouring the next day. It was about 9:30, and he was desperately exhausted. Then a pickup pulled up, and a friend got out and said, "The Lord told me to come and help you." Together, illuminated by the pickup headlights, they finished the job.

Another time, a women's Bible study decided to do more than pray for a member hospitalized with mental problems. They knew her home was as chaotic as her mind. With her husband's permission, they gave her home a top-to-bottom cleaning and reorganization, helping her have a fresh start when released.

Stooping: Splendor in the Ordinary

Our family has two standard jokes of the worst things that can happen in life. One is Mom cooking liver and onions for dinner. The other is getting stuck with cleaning the bathrooms. Liver hasn't happened in years, but I specialize in the sanitary duty. This surprises people who, learning that I've written several books, look at me with glazed awe. But the Lord can be honored by bathroom cleaners as well as by preachers or writers. I've never forgotten the story told of a young man attending a Bible school in the Philippines. He didn't think the bathrooms were clean enough, so he complained to the school's president. A little later, to his amazement, he saw the president slip out of his office with a mop and pail and enter the restroom to clean it himself. "It was a major lesson to me on being a servant," the young man said.[2] German pastor Dietrich Bonhoeffer remarked in *Life Together* that Christians need to learn how to manifest "active helpfulness" or "simple assistance in trifling, external matters." Whenever people live together, he added, there are all sorts of these needs and nobody should consider himself too important to do them. "One who worries about the loss of time that such petty, outward acts of encouragement entail," he said, "is usually taking the importance of his own career too solemnly."[3]

Ruth willingly and literally stooped to help Naomi. Hour after hour in the hot sun, she bent over to gather stalks left by harvesters. Since the famine's scarcities were still fresh memories in the minds of the harvesters, I suspect they weren't very generous about spilling stalks, despite Levitical law requiring it as their form of welfare. But they quickly noticed Ruth's diligence. By break time, when the owner came from town to greet his workers, she was the talk of the field. They reported that she'd "worked steadily from morning until now, except for a short rest in the shelter" (Ruth 2:7).

There's little glamour in the ministry of helping. You commit yourself to ordinary and sometimes exhausting jobs. But they're tasks that bless people. One of the most appreciated acts of service is housework. Frances remembers how, after her father's death, her mother's church friends showed up at the door with rubber gloves, mops, buckets, and mending supplies. "We're your friendly cleaning ladies," they said, plunging in to renew a house neglected during a long illness. A few years later, Frances cared for her sister until she died. Again the housework suffered, but, sadly, no one came to help. "When faced with the disaster area I called my home, I felt overwhelmed by the task of putting it all back together," she said. "That was the most depressing and difficult thing I had to do related to [my sister's] illness and death."[4]

We don't have to turn a house upside-down to encourage. Little tasks are long remembered. Four decades later, Verna still remembers the traumatic time when she was a teenager and her mother was hospitalized with a nervous breakdown. During those days before permanent press clothing, her former Sunday school teacher visited several times to do the family's ironing. Meal and cleaning assignments spread out among many church friends encouraged Fred when his wife had an affair, abandoning him and their four children. A close relative said he almost gave up on life, but those meals delivered two and three times a week reminded him that people really cared.

Child care also qualifies. A divorcing friend told me how much it meant when people took her children for a few hours, just to give her time alone as she worked through her emotional upheaval and the exhaustion of being a single parent. I remember how encouraged I was near the end of my second pregnancy when a friend took my toddler to her home so I could sleep. When she brought Zach back— happy from the royal treatment at her home—I found she'd tucked homemade cookies into his diaper bag. Another woman, struggling with cancer, appreciated those who offered to baby-sit, even when she and her husband stayed home. That gave them privacy to be together as a couple while they coped with her illness.

"Outdoor" needs count, too. Mary and Carlton will never forget the friend who showed up one winter night with his snowblower to clear their driveway—a job impossible for Carlton right after heart bypass surgery. An eighty-year-old widow who lived alone was encouraged by a man who came weekly to mow her lawn and also take time to sip some tea and visit with her. Another couple looked forward to the autumn Saturday every year when a mom and two kids from their church raked up more than a dozen bags of leaves—a task the couple's health wouldn't allow. "It was fun for us," the mother said. "The kids loved raking up the big leaf mountain and jumping into it before we bagged it all. We don't have big trees, so this was a treat. Plus it helped teach my kids to serve others."

So many tasks can become encouragement. My dad boosted others as a "tinkerer" who loved to redeem broken things at his workbench. My mother served by helping people with sewing projects and mending. Paula, another single, encouraged me when she arranged her vacations to help me drive on three long-distance moves before I married. As I cleaned out my parents' home after their deaths, college friends Judy and Arlene came 150 miles to help me sort clothes and do other emotionally difficult jobs. Pam, whom I barely knew, came over one morning to help me paint the living room of my parents' home. It was a tremendous boost, since I was so tired from painting many other rooms myself.

For many years I've shared with people moving to our town a handout I developed called "Newcomer's Hints." It provides local information ranging from children's library story hour to Farmer's Market hours to where they can buy "blemished" shoes for half-price. Sometimes I've driven my new-to-town friends around for a couple of hours, pointing out important stores and helping them get a feel for the town map. In later years they frequently mentioned how helpful the tips and trip were—and how welcomed they felt by that simple service.

Helping is also a ministry we can teach our children. My children have grown up participating in ministries of yardwork or baby-sitting. They've seen me mend, sew, type papers, or cut hair for others. They've watched their dad help friends move or change the oil on a single mom's car. I knew this training was taking hold one fall day when I missed seeing Zach, then fifteen, around the house. Calling outside, I found him next door at Grandma's, raking her leaves at his own initiative. He's also gotten up at 6 A.M. to shovel her walks after a snowstorm. And my kids have ministered to me. One beastly hot summer I got involved in painting Grandma's house. Anxious to paint in the cool of the morning, I was out before 7 A.M. while the kids, too young to be on paint ladders, slept in. By 11:30 I dragged into the house to find they'd made me lunch (a peanut butter sandwich) and set it on our red "You Are Special" plate! I was so encouraged I could have painted another hour in that 100-degree weather.

Let God Synergize

Every decade has its "in" word, such as *prioritize* or *economize*. Recently we had *synergize*. When I first heard that term, I thought it described something that washers did on spin cycle. Then I borrowed a book on habits of highly effective people from my highly effective neighbor, Terri. I read it in snatches of time during carpool runs and then promptly lost it! A few days later it surfaced at Grandma's house, where I'd put it down to haul her garbage to the curb. I finally got to the end and learned that effective people have learned the secret of "synergizing." In other words, when they allow individual efforts to come together in a project, they find the result is bigger than the sum of efforts by themselves. I look at it like yeast in bread dough. Put a little yeast in a blob of flour, sugar, water, and oil, and you've got action!

God seems to delight in working that way. When we offer him a little service, he takes it and truly blesses it. You see that in the book of Ruth as Boaz heard of her helper's heart and desire to encourage his relative Naomi. "May the Lord repay you for what you have done," he said. "May you be richly rewarded by the Lord, the God of Israel, under whose wings you have come to take refuge" (Ruth 2:12). Boaz made sure that happened. He offered her some lunch from his own picnic basket. Then, while she was out of earshot, he told his helpers to make sure they left extra gleanings for her to pick up. As a result, that day she took home more than half a bushel of barley—enough to support her and Naomi for five days. Boaz gave Ruth his blessing to stay with him all through the harvest, assuring her of enough gleanings to live on.

Of course, the grander story was that Boaz turned out to be Ruth and Naomi's "kinsman-redeemer." By marrying Ruth, he kept the inheritance in Naomi's family. By him, Ruth also bore a son who became an ancestor of King David and of Jesus Christ.

Who would have thought it of two lonely, impoverished women, staggering into little Bethlehem one dusty spring day? Only God, in his wonderful way of synergizing and exploding our simple acts of service.

Janet experienced that during one overwhelming year in her life. It started when her third baby, Nicholas, was four months old. Noting unusual lethargy, droopy eyes, and a lack of appetite, she took him to the doctor. Her son was diagnosed with a rare and sometimes fatal disease, airborne infant botulism. Hospitalized, he got progressively weaker. A feeding tube was installed. Then one day he stopped breathing and had to be resuscitated. He was put on a ventilator and rushed to a city hospital 150 miles away.

Janet was beside herself. The day Nicholas stopped breathing, her daughter, Rachel, was starting kindergarten. Her other son, Brent, was two. The crisis was simply too big for Janet and her husband to cope with alone. But God stepped in, using people and the synergy of encouragement in its various forms. Her relatives took her other children into their homes. As she stayed by her critically ill son's crib, Janet received cards and letters nearly every day. Her Bible study friends sent over a big wicker basket of snack foods, magazines, books, phone cards, and cash. Others sent money to pay for rent in special housing for patients' families.

When Nicholas improved enough to return to the local hospital for care while the disease ran its course, the ministry of service kicked in full time. For two months, Janet's friends brought the family meals approximately every other day. "I just left the key hidden outside for them," she says. "Most of the time I didn't even know who left food. But those meals took an incredible load off my mind. After focusing my days and energy on Nicholas at the hospital, I simply didn't have enough of me left to worry about shopping and cooking."

Just before Christmas, some older women from another

Bible study gave Janet's home a preholiday cleaning and left a good supply of Christmas cookies. They also decorated, provided little gifts for her children, and gave her and her husband a certificate for a dinner out alone.

When Nicholas finally came home after Christmas, he was still very ill, requiring a feeding tube. Friends stayed on twenty-four-hour alert, as Janet's days were filled with his appointments with doctors and therapists. One day she mentioned to her mom how much her home needed a thorough spring cleaning—a task she'd lacked time or energy to do since Nicholas's birth the previous year. Her parents were then working with retired, itinerant Christian builders called "Sowers" on a church project about an hour and a half drive away. The Sowers' wives, hearing the need, decided to act.

"One day nine Sowers ladies showed up at my door," Janet remembers. "They worked for eight hours—washing windows, walls, doors, cupboards, and bathrooms. They vacuumed and dusted, stripped and waxed my kitchen floor. It would have taken me a year to do all that. I still cry to think about all their loving work."

Janet says at first it was hard for her to accept all the help and encouragement she received through Nicholas's time of illness. "I guess it was an ego thing," she says. "But I came to realize that this was how God wanted to provide for us. These people, through meals and cleaning and other means of encouragement, were God's messengers of love."

Nicholas is eating again and "catching up" developmentally from spending most of his first year of life seriously ill. But his mother will never be the same as she encounters other people in crisis situations. "I've learned how these are times our service can give glory to God," she said.

An old hymn by Washington Gladden begins:

> O Master, let me walk with Thee
> in lowly paths of service free;

> tell me Thy secret; help me bear
> the strain of toil, the fret of care.

We show we walk with the Master when we help bear others' burdens, even in simple tasks. The late Dawson Trotman, founder of The Navigators, once hiked with a Taiwanese pastor into a remote mountain village to meet with national Christians. The roads and trails were wet, and they arrived with very muddy shoes. When someone later asked the pastor what he remembered of Trotman, he replied without hesitation, "He cleaned my shoes." This humble pastor was surprised and awed that the Christian leader from America woke before him and wiped off his shoes.[5]

People will long remember a spirit of service. The trowel is a powerful weapon among the weeds of discouragement.

Groomed to Bloom

1. Mark 15:41 reveals that even Jesus accepted the encouragement of service. If you'd been one of the women in this passage, what would you have done?
2. The greatest example of servanthood came from Jesus in the upper room. Read John 13:1-17 and tell how he showed "the full extent of his love" (v. 1). Why do you think he also washed Judas's feet?
3. Some people think some acts of service are more honorable or important than are others. What does 1 Corinthians 12:21-26 say about that?
4. Do you ever grumble about having to help somebody? What checks do you get from the last instruction of Romans 12:8 and the last half of 1 Peter 4:11?
5. This memory verse will remind you of the focus of service: "Whatever you do, work at it with all your heart, as working for the Lord, not for men" (Col. 3:23).

10
Rock Gardeners

The Training of the Encourager

Out here in lands birthed by volcanoes, we dream about Real Soil. We've heard of places where soil is so rich you sink a shovel through it as easily as a knife through hot butter. You fling seeds at it, and before you can whistle "Mississippi Mud" ten times, you have a harvest. The rest of us must cope with rocks, sweat, and tears.

For several years I tried to grow a garden. I'd hoe-hoe-hoe along until I'd hear that telltale "chink" and dig up a big gray potato shape where I hadn't planted potatoes. After repeated pitches of those teeth-breaking "inedibles" to left field, I built quite a mound.

It took me a few years, but now I realize why so many people in these parts have rock gardens: we have the raw materials for those horticultural delights in abundance. People who want nice lawns pay to have soil brought in. Otherwise, you sentence yourself to the same activity that used to occupy prison chain gangs.

What a picture of real life comes from rock gardens! In *When I Got on the Highway to Heaven, I Didn't Expect Rocky Roads,* I told about people who trusted God in difficult life experiences. They used rocks as stepping stones, not stumbling blocks. We all will experience rocky roads in life. God never promised us a rose garden, nor fields of heather, nor ivory towers. But this is why we have encouragement. When we find ourselves literally between a rock and another hard place, when we experience sorrow and distress, we may think of ourselves as a pile of barren rocks. But during those times the Lord, through the ministry of encouragement, pulls out the weeds and gently tucks rock-hugging plants into the little pockets of soil. His "assistants" in this work know just what to do because they, too, once experienced the rocks of life. If we have been encouraged, we learn to be encouragers.

This principle is fleshed out in the story of a New Testament seamstress named Dorcas. Most people remember her as the nimble-needled lady who got a second chance to live. But there are deeper dimensions to her story to encourage us in our own journeys as encouragers:

- The ministry of encouragement comes with spiritual growth.
- Encouragement grows out of ordinary skills.
- God is there—even in our deepest distress.
- We'd be surprised how God uses us.
- The greatest encouragement is our hope of eternal life.

Growing into Encouragers

My late mother belonged to a "Dorcas Circle," which turned fabric scraps into quilts and lap robes. It was a natural outlet for Mom, who lived and breathed sewing and wore out two sewing machines. One day she was so preoccupied with sewing that she told a gas station attendant, "Four yards of gas, please." With "sew" much of this in my background, it's natural that I'd be drawn to the biography of Dorcas, known for sewing for the needy. As I searched out her biography in Acts 9:36-42, I realized how this woman truly allowed God to bring encouragement out of difficult circumstances.

Her name (Dorcas in Greek, Tabitha in Aramaic) meant "gazelle" or "doe," referring to a small antelope known for its beauty and speed, and the subject of much poetry in her time. The name was appropriate for this particular seamstress, the lady who was "Speedy for the Needy." But her most important character trait is revealed in an innocent phrase of verse 36: "there was a disciple named Dorcas." The Greek word for "disciple" used there is *mathetria*, meaning a female disciple. This word and its male counterpart denoted a learner, someone who imitated his teacher.

Scripture doesn't name the teacher who brought the good news about Jesus Christ to Joppa, the little seaport where Dorcas lived, thirty-five miles northwest of Jerusalem. Peter's first recorded visit came after she died. Perhaps some of those who fled for their lives during the post-Pentecost persecutions went to Joppa and led others to Christ, including Dorcas. More important than the teacher's identity was the result: she turned her heart and vocation over to the Lord and made a difference where she lived.

People continue to make a difference where they live. Obituaries in our small-town newspaper list for some people extensive club memberships and community honors. But when I skim those "obits," I find myself looking for evidence that a person made the eternal, spiritual difference. A church membership doesn't always mean a person was a Christian. But sometimes a family—perhaps at the request of the person who was dying—will add a sentence remarking that the most important element in the deceased's life was his or her relationship to Jesus Christ. We can "do good" until our lives are reduced to obituary. But it won't matter for eternity if we don't know Christ. A lot of people think mistakenly that they'll get to heaven on the basis of their good works. But the Bible clearly denies that. Ephesians 2:8 says we're saved—granted a relationship with God through forgiveness of sins—"by faith." We have the hope of eternal life when we believe that Christ indeed died for us. "Not by works," adds verse 9, "so that no one can boast." "Works" come later as we express our faith in obeying God. Verse 10 says we were "created in Christ

Jesus to do good works, which God prepared in advance for us to do." But good works by themselves are not the way to heaven.

For years I struggled with that concept. I grew up in a church where the Ten Commandments and the Beatitudes were faithfully taught. But I didn't connect the Gospel accounts of Jesus' dying on the cross with my personal need for forgiveness of sins. I thought if I were "good enough," I'd somehow get God's approval and make it to heaven. How wrong I was. I was a young adult before I realized I needed to humble myself before God, forget about my "works" list, and simply accept that he loved me enough to send Jesus to die on my behalf.

When I did that, I entered God's family. Day after day, year by year, I have been acquiring that celestial "family resemblance." We're born with physical resemblance to our parents (my kids got my thick eyebrows and overbite). When we're born into the family of God, he wants us to become more and more like Jesus—more loving, patient, kind, and generous. As we grow into the role of encouragers, we're simply becoming like Christ to the world around us. This was what made Dorcas so special. She truly knew how to love people because she had experienced Christ's love. Then, as today, individuals and philanthropic organizations could pass out food and clothes, but only Christians could offer the hope that comes from knowing Jesus Christ. Sharing the Lord makes the important difference.

Disciples need the spiritual equivalent of soil, water, and sunlight. We need hearts weeded out, plowed soft, and receptive to the Lord. We need Christ the Living Water to pour over us, cleansing us and refreshing us. We need to let the love of God reflect in our lives. All these come through fellowship, prayer, and studying God's Word.

The Bible clearly links fellowship with encouragement. "Let us not give up meeting together, as some are in the habit of doing," says Hebrews 10:25, "but let us encourage one another—and all the more as you see the Day approaching." Even the early church had people who got lazy about getting together with other Christians. But the writer of Hebrews knew how important it was for them to come together, to encourage each other in their spiritual walk, and to anticipate the prophesied, coming day when Jesus will come again. That's why I look forward to church, Bible study, retreats, and just talking with vibrant Christian friends. They keep me focused.

Prayer and personal Bible study also keep our hearts encouraged and keep us in training as "encouragers." People who limit their intake of God's Word to Sunday sermons and quickie devotional books are like children who grab a soft drink and doughnut for breakfast. It just won't hold you. As a young Christian I was taught to read the Bible regularly, thoughtfully, and daily. I was encouraged to write in a journal what a passage was teaching me. I even learned it was okay to mark up my Bible. That was radical permission for someone who grew up thinking writing in her Bible was as sacrilegious as Uzzah's touching the Ark of the Covenant (2 Sam. 6:6-7). My attitude changed when I got into a church with people who actually took their Bibles and used them during the sermon! None of that sanitary "today's lesson is printed on the back of the bulletin" stuff. Their Bibles held evidence to convict them of being Christians. Some held virtual commentaries, up and down the columns. They made me feel sorry for the minister who might do their funerals—if his habit was to hold up the deceased's Bible and comment on passages he found highlighted or underlined. That funeral sermon could have gone on for hours!

Another spiritual discipline that can help people grow as encouragers is Scripture memorization. There's nothing like getting a few of the Bible's eight hundred promises into your heart to help you anticipate what God can bring out of difficulties. I began with the Topical Memory Program published by The Navigators, then launched out on my own on selected verses, writing them out on three-by-five cards. The verses I chose reflected the particular needs for encouragement that I had at that time in my life. One year I memorized all of Romans 8. Within the next two years both my parents had died. Having memorized that chapter helped my heart claim God's promise that absolutely nothing—not even death—could separate me from his love. Plus, it reaffirmed Romans 8:28, that all this would work together for good. Sometimes, verses I've memorized will come to mind when God has assigned me to encourage someone else. When God's Word is part of my heart, then I truly can be the messenger of his consolation and hope. Like Dorcas, I can be a disciple reaching out to others.

The Ordinary Becoming Extraordinary

Little is said about Dorcas's financial circumstances or marital status. She may have been widowed but apparently had enough financial comfort to enable her to be "always doing good and helping the poor" (Acts 9:36). Some conjectured that Dorcas took her sewing basket upstairs to her flat roof in the early evening to catch the cooling coastal breezes. From there she had a seagull's view of people walking the streets, many of whom were destitute after losing husbands and fathers who were fishermen to the ocean's winds and rocks. Rather than just despair, Dorcas became part of the solution. Stitch by stitch, she hand-fashioned each garment. Then she personally delivered them to these fatherless homes, taking time to encourage the widows in the Lord.

We carry on the legacy of Dorcas when we get involved in situations that are bigger than we are. Dr. Bob Pierce, founder of World Vision, had this prayer written on the flyleaf of his dilapidated Bible: "Let my heart be broken with the things that break the heart of God."[1] When we let our hearts be broken, we get our hands dirty, nudging little plants of encouragement into the niches of soil amidst the rocks of adversity. We might think our efforts will never be noticed, but they will. Plant by plant, the pile will become a piece of beauty.

Such was the experience of Donise when her husband, Jim, had risky surgery on a degenerating spinal cord. Without the procedure, he'd eventually become paralyzed. The high-tech surgery at a hospital 150 miles away from home went well; then complications required a second surgery. Problems with Jim's remaining conscious, plus pneumonia, compounded the gravity of his condition. Within days, an army of "Dorcases" embraced their need.

"We'd left our children with friends, never imagining we'd be away for more than three weeks," Donise said. "I didn't want to be a burden on anybody, and I suspected keeping my kids and tending to their extras like piano lessons added a lot of stress to those families' lives. But when I was going through this crisis with Jim, it meant so much to have people assure me that keeping our kids was no problem. It enabled me to focus on Jim and decisions I had to make in this emergency."

The ministries of written and spoken words, prayer, and presence brought hope to Donise as she waited at Jim's bedside in critical care. The father of Jim's secretary offered hospitality "in absentia" by allowing Donise to stay at his home while he was away, even though they'd never met. Back home, besides taking care of her children, people expressed the encouragement of service by shoveling her walks and driveways and gathering her mail, staying alert for bills Donise needed sent to her for payment. As Jim's problems continued, friends suggested flying the children to be with their mother. One person even offered to cover the airfare if the family finances were too lean.

"Their timing was God's," Donise said. "I thought this might be too extravagant, but they persuaded me to have the children come. A few hours after they got to their dad's bedside, Jim woke up and from then on made rapid improvement."

One woman told Donise: "God's telling me to make helping your family a priority in my life as long as Jim has these health problems." This touched Donise tremendously. "This person always has projects going," Donise said, "and here she was willing to put them aside, just for us."

When Jim came home, a friend brought a "welcome home" meal and a pumpkin pie. Jim smiled broadly when the pie was delivered, since pumpkin was not only a favorite pie but also one whose flavor he could truly taste despite postsurgical dulling of taste buds. "I just thought it would be soft for him to eat with his neck in a brace," the friend remarked.

As Jim recovered at home, he and Donise realized that even more people had supported them through this difficult experience. People they hardly knew greeted them at church and said, "I prayed for you."

"I still cry to think about how people anticipated our needs and went into action," Donise said. "It was like Jesus looked down and saw me engulfed in a crisis so big and overwhelming that I couldn't handle it myself. So he spoke to people on my behalf to help us through it. This was truly the body of Christ at work."

God's Presence in Our Deepest Distress

The love Dorcas expressed to her town was returned when she died. They washed her body and placed it in an upstairs room, then sent for the most influential church leader they knew: Peter, preaching in Lydda, eleven miles southeast. Perhaps they hoped against hope that Peter could plead with God to raise Dorcas from the dead. Word had already spread how he'd healed the paralytic Aeneas. Or maybe they simply acted out of overwhelming distress over the gap left in the spiritual community by her death.

Blunt, action-oriented Peter must have been rather astonished when he was led into a room full of weeping widows, their arms full of garments she'd made for them and their children. Peter was no stranger to miracles. He'd experienced Pentecost. He'd seen people healed and freed of demons. But the Lord had used none of the disciples to raise someone from the dead. Peter came beside this woman's cold body, got on his knees and prayed, then declared, "Tabitha, get up." She opened her eyes and sat up, and he helped her to her feet. Then he called all the believers and widows into her room. They knew how dead she'd been! The reversal of her death turned Joppa upside-down, and many believed in the Lord.

At some time in our lives, and often several times, each of us will experience a distress that we think can't get any deeper. An illness, accident, or loss strips us of all that is familiar and comfortable. We reach the end of our resources. We wonder if God is really watching or if he really cares. We find ourselves barely able to pray, struggling to trust, wondering if there is really hope. Then God breaks into our gloom with a reminder that he is still there in our deepest distress. This verse from the old hymn "How Firm a Foundation" says it well:

> When through the deep waters I call thee to go,
> the rivers of sorrow shall not overflow;
> for I will be with thee, thy trials to bless
> and sanctify to thee thy deepest distress.

Life is not one steadily ascending rocky road. It's one that goes up hills and down into valleys, up again, down again, before it finally reaches our heavenly destination. Every time we climb out of a valley with the Lord's help, we are stronger for climbing out of the next.

That's what my friends Randy and Debby are discovering. They had been married a few years when compounded sorrows entered their lives. Both sets of parents divorced. A close grandmother died. But Randy and Debby were expecting their first baby. They hoped this new life would bring some healing to their hurt.

Debby was seven months pregnant when her doctor measured her stomach and suspected a problem. He ordered an ultrasound. The news was not good. Her baby—a little boy—had only one kidney, already believed impaired by a large cyst. Grief washed over their lives before the baby was even born. They hoped for the best but braced for the worst.

After a difficult labor and delivery, during which Debby experienced life-threatening bleeding, Daniel Paul was born with multiple problems. His head was enlarged from edema of the weak kidney. He had club feet and, worse, defects throughout his elimination system. He was only hours old when he was airlifted to a special children's hospital 150 miles away. There, surgeons performed an emergency colostomy and began other measures to help him survive.

The next weeks were clouded with uncertainties, pain, and loneliness as Daniel's parents kept vigil by his crib in neonatal intensive care. But encouragement also sent its strong, warm shafts through those clouds of despair.

There were presence and touch as people simply showed up with caring hugs, even hours from home and in a crowded urban area. If Debby wasn't there—if she'd taken a break to eat or sleep—they left notes for her. Some visitors embodied 2 Corinthians 1, comforting as they had once been comforted in their own experiences with birth defects. One had known cleft palate, another, spina bifida.

"It meant so much to see familiar faces," Debby said. "I not only had a very sick baby facing lifelong complications; I'd been ripped from my home. I had to sleep in a strange room and interact with strangers. I really needed those links with home."

Letters and phone calls added the written and spoken dimensions of encouragement, as Debby recalled: "I appreciated having somebody tell me how my flowers were doing, what was happening in town, and what the pastor preached on."

And there were prayers. Debby says sometimes her anguish was so great that she couldn't find the words to lift up to God. "That's when people stood in the gap for us," she said. "I felt so helpless, a mother who couldn't even pray for her own child. But I had a real sense of being buoyed up as people interceded for us."

Service and giving also entered their lives as Daniel was released to intensive home care. Friends celebrated his birth, three months later, with a shower.

During Daniel's first year of life, he underwent eighteen major and minor surgeries. Some of them resulted in infections serious enough for intravenous antibiotics. Then came the surgery that assaulted Daniel's ability to survive. One day as Debby held him at the hospital, he stopped breathing. Debby screamed for help, and nurses hurriedly led her away as personnel converged on him to revive him.

"Oh God, he's yours," Debby prayed through her tears. So many times that had been the prayer of her heart, but this time the emergency made that prayer so real and so hard. Then she sensed the heaviness in the room lift. There was a laughter of relief, the small talk of success, and they summoned her back to her baby. As she walked back to his crib, a light beamed right down on his bed like a divine spotlight on a piece of God's glory. Daniel was breathing again, and Debby realized again that God was there—in her deepest distress.

Surprises at Debriefing

A missionary nurse from our church often used Ray Boltz's song "Thank You for Giving to the Lord" to accompany her slides of the patients and people she served in central Haiti. It always gripped me to see those soulful brown eyes, big toothy smiles, and weathered gray hands in her photos. When the lyrics talked about the fruits of giving to missions or faithfully teaching Sunday school, I realized again how someday we'll meet a host of people whose lives we touched without realizing it.

Dorcas was unusually privileged. She got to know what people thought of her after she died! I'm sure she was quite amazed as she woke up to a crowd of needy people clutching the clothing she'd sewn to encourage them. No doubt she heard reports of what was said about her as she lay dead and cold. Scripture records no more of Dorcas's story after she was raised back to life, but I think it must have been quite a story. Probably her ministry of sewing increased in fervor and faith until the Lord said again in her old age, "Come home to heaven!"

I think God will have a lot of surprises for us as he opens up the accounts revealing how we encouraged others in his name. There may be some lives touched when we thought we didn't have anything in us to give out. In her weeks at the hospital, Debby was so worn out and preoccupied with baby Daniel that she simply couldn't focus on ministry. Yet she realizes she did reach out to other parents in crisis, even if it meant just telling them where they could shower or recommending a teriyaki place down the street. In later months, as they returned to that hospital complex for follow-up, she made that extra effort to return to the hospital floor where he'd spent his most critical hours and show the nurses how he'd progressed. "They told me they don't often see these babies after they leave the hospital," Debby said. "It encouraged them to know he was making it okay."

Life's Greatest Encouragement

If we spend a lot of time in the valleys, we sometimes forget what the mountain looks like. In Washington's Puyallup Valley, where I grew up, the rainy climate means many gray days. Clouds often block views of the most spectacular scenic attraction, Mount Rainier. On sunny days, I'd walk to the end of our street to see if the mountain "was out." In local lingo, that meant you could see it from its royal throne of foothills forty miles away. I was always thrilled to see that big lump of vanilla ice cream in the distance.

I hope we never tire of waiting to see something even greater: the return of the Lord Jesus. This was the number-one booster shot for the New Testament church. When life got rough, their leaders would remind them that someday the dead who loved Jesus will explode from their graves with new bodies and be zapped to the clouds to meet the Lord in the air. And right behind them, Christians still living would be whisked up for that incredible reunion. "And so we will be with the Lord forever," the apostle Paul wrote. "Therefore encourage each other with these words" (1 Thess. 4:17-18). He also wrote Titus: "We wait for the blessed hope—the glorious appearing of our great God and Savior, Jesus Christ" (Titus 2:13).

Encourage one another with these words. We don't do enough of it. It's true we're not to be so heavenly minded that we're of no earthly good. But to be of earthly good, we need to be heavenly minded and live in the excitement and assurance that something better is truly guaranteed. The second coming of Christ will outdo any human celebrations. New Year's Eve on Times Square will be a dead firecracker in comparison. Halftime at the Super Bowl will be a swim party in a kids' inflatable pool. All the presidential inauguration hoopla will be a skip around the block. The glorious consummation of God's plan for all ages—the return of his Son to reign with all the promises of a new heaven and a new earth—will be so amazing that we have no words to even try to anticipate it. Except . . . "encourage one another with these words."

In one sense, we're anticipating that event as we buy thousands of novels that guess at what might happen in the days leading to Christ's return. We're showing our nervous curiosity about the afterlife when we publicize the stories of people who clinically died and were revived. Had Dorcas lived today, I'm sure that journalists and researchers would have stormed her door. Did she experience a "tunnel" sensation? a glowing light? music? a compelling, friendly presence? We're not told, and I contend it really doesn't matter. Our hope is not based on a supernatural experience but on the Word of God. We can affirm with hymn writer Edward Mote:

> My hope is built on nothing less
> than Jesus' blood and righteousness.

The last verse proclaims:

> When He shall come with trumpet sound,
> O may I then in Him be found;
> dressed in His righteousness alone,
> faultless to stand before the throne.

Have you come to that point in your life where you know that you can stand before God without shame? Where you know that the encouraging promise of heaven is yours?

As one of my former pastors, whom we called "Pastor D," went through a long losing battle with heart disease, he was able to ask many of his caregivers those questions. One chaplain intern, while visiting Pastor D in his last weeks, mentioned that she "hoped" she had settled things appropriately with God. Pastor D replied, "My dear, you can *know* you have settled things with God. Let me tell you what to do." And then this dying man did what he had done hundreds of times before: he helped her pray to become a Christian.

The chorus of Mote's hymn affirms:

> On Christ, the solid Rock, I stand;
> all other ground is sinking sand.

Gardens planted around the solid Rock will bloom forever. Their beauty will be unsurpassed. Isaiah says the Lord will look with compassion on our ruins. He will make our wastelands like the garden of the Lord. "Joy and gladness will be found in her," says Isaiah 51:3, "thanksgiving and the sound of singing."

In our church, there's great hoopla and applause when parents show up with their days-old newborns. Debby missed that when Daniel was whisked away at birth to another hospital. One night in the hospital parent housing, in the midst of her homesickness, Debby imagined showing their son to the church family as the pastor said, "Daniel's home," and the choir sang the anthem by Tom Fettke, "The Majesty and Glory of Your Name." Debby told no one about that little imagined scene. A month later, Daniel was released. The next day was Mother's Day, and Debby and Randy sneaked late into church with their fragile little son, finding seats in the back row of the balcony. The choir was singing "The Majesty and Glory of your Name." Then the pastor got up and said, "I heard a rumor that Daniel Paul Martin is here." Applause and praise to God—and tears—followed these young parents as they made their way to the front of the church.

That's the bottom line of encouragement: the majesty and glory of God's Name. When we are rooted in him, we bloom where we are planted. And, oh, the glory of the garden where Jesus is proclaimed!

Groomed to Bloom

1. The world tries to patch up problems, but sometimes God leaves us with unpatchable problems. What hope does he provide in 2 Corinthians 12:9?
2. When Navigators' founder, Dawson Trotman, drowned after saving someone else in a lake, *Time* magazine characterized this Christian leader as "always holding somebody up." Who can you "hold up" today for Christ? Who holds you up? See Romans 5:6 and offer a prayer over this truth.
3. One way that God "sanctifies" our deepest distress is explained in 2 Corinthians 1:3-7. Write this in your own words and describe a time when it has been true of your life.

4. At the end of Winston Churchill's funeral in 1965, a lone trumpet aired the heart-catching notes of "The Last Post." Then a cavalry trumpeter answered with "Reveille." What symbolism does this recall? Find encouragement in Hebrews 10:19-25 and 1 Thessalonians 4:13-18.

5. This verse says it all: "May the God who gives endurance and encouragement give you a spirit of unity among yourselves as you follow Christ Jesus, so that with one heart and mouth you may glorify the God and Father of our Lord Jesus Christ" (Rom. 15:5-6).

Notes

Chapter 1: Barney Blooms

1. Dietrich Bonhoeffer, *Life Together,* trans. John Doberstein (New York: Harper & Row, 1954) 106.

Chapter 2: The Bent Bloom Cure

1. John W. Alexander, *Managing Our Work,* rev. ed. (Downers Grove, Ill.: InterVarsity, 1975) 53.
2. Dorothy C. Briggs, *Your Child's Self-Esteem* (Garden City, N.Y.: Doubleday, 1970) 92.
3. Franklin Graham, *Rebel with a Cause* (Nashville: Thomas Nelson, 1995) 309.
4. John W. Alexander, *Practical Criticism* (Downers Grove, Ill.: Inter-Varsity, 1975) 20-21.

Chapter 3: Living Up to the Label

1. Dr. and Mrs. Howard Taylor, *Hudson Taylor's Spiritual Secret* (London: China Inland Mission, 1950) 107.
2. Donald Bubna with Sue Multanen, "The Encouragement Card," *Leadership* 1 (Fall 1980): 52-53.
3. Donald Bubna, *Building People* (Wheaton, IL: Tyndale, 1978) 78-79.
4. Rhonda Wehler, "Creative Kindness 101," *Christian Single* (November 1996): 38.

Chapter 4: Quiet! Garden at Work!

1. Dorothy Gurney, cited in *Oxford Dictionary of Quotations,* 3rd ed. (Oxford: Oxford University Press, 1979) 237.
2. Jerry Bridges, *The Practice of Godliness* (Colorado Springs, CO: NavPress, 1983) 240.
3. Bonhoeffer 97.
4. Joe Bayly, *The Last Thing We Talk About* (London: Scripture Union, 1973) 40-41.
5. Keith Miller and Bruce Larson, *The Passionate People* (Waco, TX: Word, 1979) 42.

6. Frances Edwards Dye, "Helping in the Face of Death," *Discipleship Journal* 28 (1985): 35.

7. Paul Tournier, quoted in Miller and Larson 53.

Chapter 5: Hugging Cacti

1. Tom McNichol, "The Power of Touch," *USA Weekend* 6-8 (Feb 1998): 22.

2. Darrin Lehman with John Ellard and Camille Wortman, "Social Support for the Bereaved: Recipients' and Providers' Perspectives on What Is Helpful," *Journal on Consulting and Clinical Psychology* 53.4 (1985): 438-46.

3. McNichol 22.

4. Marilyn Willett Heavilin, *December's Song* (San Bernardino, CA: Here's Life, 1988) 89.

5. Lauren Saul, "Caring in Christ's Name," *Decision* (February 1986): 10.

6. Bubna 83.

Chapter 6: Trumpet Flower Time

1. Oswald Chambers, *Prayer: A Holy Occupation* (Grand Rapids: Discovery House, 1992) 137.

2. Richard D. Foster, *The Ministry of Encouragement* (Colorado Springs: The Challenge, n.d.) 4-5.

3. Rosalind Rinker, *Communicating Love through Prayer* (Grand Rapids: Zondervan, 1966) 53.

Chapter 7: Anything Grows

1. W. E. Vine, *An Expository Dictionary of New Testament Words* (Old Tappan, NJ: Revell, 1940) 235.

Chapter 8: Lotza Zuc to Share

1. Rick Yohn, *Discover Your Spiritual Gift and Use It* (Wheaton, IL: Tyndale, 1974) 15.

2. Fred Smith, "Something I Learned from Maxey Jarman," *Leadership* 2 (Winter 1981): 93.

3. Ethel May Baldwin and David V. Benson, *Henrietta Mears and How She Did It* (Glendale, CA: Regal, 1966) 172.

4. Anne Ortlund, *Up with Worship* (Glendale, CA: Gospel Light, 1975), pp. 119-20.

Chapter 9: Have Trowel, Will Travel

1. "The Good Samaritans," *Christianity Today* 29 (March 1974): 39.
2. Karen Mains, *Open Heart, Open Home* (Elgin, IL: Cook, 1976) 63.
3. Bonhoeffer 99.
4. Dye 35.
5. Jerry Bridges, "Loving by Serving," *Discipleship Journal* 27 (1985): 19.

Chapter 10: Rock Gardeners

1. Ted Engstrom, "Unconditional Love: The Key to Caring," *Discipleship Journal* 27 (1985): 25.